The "Higher Law" Background

OF

American Constitutional Law

BY EDWARD S. CORWIN

Cornell Paperbacks

Cornell University Press

ITHACA AND LONDON

Copyright 1928, 1929, by The Harvard Law Review Association. First published in the *Harvard Law Review*, XLII (1928–1929), 149–185; 365–409. Reprinted 1955 by permission.

CORNELL UNIVERSITY PRESS

Second printing 1957
Third printing 1959
Fourth printing 1961
Fifth printing 1963
Sixth printing, Cornell Paperbacks, 1965
Seventh printing 1967
Eighth printing 1971

International Standard Book Number 0-8014-9012-X

PRINTED IN THE UNITED STATES OF AMERICA
BY VALLEY OFFSET, INC.

Prefatory Note

THE hard core of the American tradition is a belief in constitutional government. When the American pledges his allegiance to democracy, as he so often must in this age that mingles triumph and frustration, he means *constitutional* democracy, a system of government in which political power is diffused by a written constitution and the wielders of power are held in check by the rule of law. In his opinion, there is no inherent conflict between democracy and constitutionalism. The latter is simply a guarantee that the former will be carried on through safe, sober, predictable methods. Since men, even the thrice-blessed Americans, can always be led into temptation and thence into corruption by the taste and touch of power, they must agree to govern themselves under self-imposed restraints or lose their freedom. And since democracy is based on common agreement to proceed slowly through discussion and compromise and to avoid bold steps that cannot be retraced, they must recognize that the complex of ideas and procedures known as "constitutionalism" strengthens rather than frustrates the democratic process.

The American, like men of other nations and cultures, expresses his most precious beliefs with the help of symbols. The symbol of his constitutionalism, and its instrument as well, is the Constitution of 1787, an ingenious catalogue of grants and limitations that is not just casually admired but diligently honored. His high regard for the Constitution, amounting often to idolatry, is explained on numerous grounds. One explanation, of course, is its source: in law the sovereign people, in fact "an assembly of demi-gods" some of whose names were Washington, Madison, Hamilton, and Franklin. Another is its age, hardly so impressive as that of Magna Carta or the Decalogue, yet greater now than that of any other charter of government anywhere in the world. Still another is its success, whether as splendid sign of freedom and unity or as tutor in the trials and blessings of ordered liberty. Yet the most compelling explanation is the American's deep-seated conviction that the Constitution is an expression of the Higher Law, that it is in fact imperfect man's most perfect rendering of what Blackstone saluted as "the eternal, immutable laws of good and evil, to which the creator himself in all his dispensations conforms; and which he has enabled human reason to discover, so far as they are necessary for the conduct of human actions." This conviction has been a dominant influence in American constitutional law almost from the day the Constitution was put into commission.

Professor Corwin's notable essay, reprinted here for the first time in almost twenty years, is an eloquent introduction to the idea of the Constitution as Higher Law. From the time it first appeared in the *Harvard Law Review* in 1928–1929,[1] this exploration of the remote sources of the American Constitution has been one of the most universally admired and heavily used essays in constitutional law and American political thought. The reasons for the continued respect in which it is held are visible on its face. It is learned: Consider the footnotes, so characteristic of Professor Corwin's scholarly offerings and so useful to the teacher and scholar. It is eloquent: Consider the magisterial handling of the celebrated Blackstone—"Nor is Blackstone's appeal to men of all parties difficult to understand. Eloquent, suave, undismayed in the presence of the palpable

[1] *Harvard Law Review*, XLII (1928–1929), 149, 365; reprinted in *Selected Essays in Constitutional Law* (Chicago, 1938), I, 1–67.

contradictions in his pages, adept in insinuating new points of view without unnecessarily disturbing old ones, he is the very exemplar and model of legalistic and judicial obscurantism." Above all, it is humbling: No one can come away from reading it without realizing how much we in America are a part of Western civilization. The men we meet in the pages of this essay—Demosthenes, Sophocles, Aristotle, Cicero, Seneca, Ulpian, Gaius, John of Salisbury, Isidore of Seville, St. Thomas Aquinas, Bracton, Fortescue, Coke, Grotius, Newton, Hooker, Pufendorf, Locke, Blackstone—all insisted that the laws by which men live can and should be the "embodiment of essential and unchanging justice," and we may salute them respectfully as founding fathers of our experiment in ordered liberty. It should do us good to remember at the height of our power and self-esteem that our political tradition and constitutional law are late blooms on a sturdy growth more than two thousand years old and still vigorous.

The rest of these few words are more likely to be tribute than introduction. It would be ungracious in a student and teacher of American political and constitutional thought to present an example of Professor Corwin's work without bespeaking the considerable debt that all of us owe this remarkable scholar. The list of his published works is sufficient evidence of the debt: I count a full twenty titles in the card catalogue of the Cornell University Library, and at least a dozen of these studies were timely and remain definitive in the best sense of those overworked adjectives. I would hardly hazard a guess as to the total number of his articles in the learned journals.

A teacher to the teachers, he has also been a scholar for the scholars, quarrying from the deep recesses of intellectual and constitutional history and laying out neatly for our confident use a mass of invaluable materials that few of us would have the time or talent to dig up for ourselves. And he has done all this with thoroughness and fidelity unsurpassed in the scholarship of American political science. Suspecting, like that prince of scholars, Otto von Gierke, that "it is not probable that for some time to come anyone will tread exactly the same road that

I have trod in long years of fatiguing toil," he has seen to it that those who retrace his steps will find the way straight and secure.

This choice essay, "The 'Higher Law' Background of American Constitutional Law," is a model of Professor Corwin's scholarship. It is presented once again to students of constitutional law and political theory for instruction and inspiration in the sources of a great American tradition.

CLINTON ROSSITER

Ithaca, New York
February, 1955

Contents

Edward S. Corwin

A Biographical Note

EDWARD S. CORWIN, historian of the Constitution, was born of old New England stock near Plymouth, Michigan, in 1878. After graduating from the University of Michigan in 1900 and winning his doctorate at the University of Pennsylvania in 1905, he was called to Princeton by Woodrow Wilson in 1905 as one of the original group of preceptors, so many of whom went on to fame as teachers and scholars. Professor Corwin taught at Princeton until his retirement in 1946. Princeton men around the world remember fondly the "rugged but excellent" course in Constitutional Interpretation taught by the McCormick Professor of Jurisprudence.

If Professor Corwin left an indelible mark on Princeton, he has left one far more indelible and influential on the theory and practice of government in the United States. American constitutional law—not just the law taught by professors, but the law debated by Senators and proclaimed by judges—has never been quite the same since first he took his incisive pen in hand. *The President's Removal Power under the Constitution* (1927), *The Twilight of the Supreme Court* (1934), *The Commerce Power versus States' Rights* (1936), *Court over Constitu-*

tion (1938), *The President: Office and Powers* (1940; rev. ed., 1948), and *The Constitution and World Organization* (1944) were books that changed the minds of men in the seats of power in Washington as in the seats of learning about the country. Nor should his other books be forgotten, certainly not *The Doctrine of Judicial Review* (1914), *The President's Control of Foreign Relations* (1917), *John Marshall and the Constitution* (1919), *Total War and the Constitution* (1947), and *Liberty against Government* (1948). All of these remain useful tools in the kit of every self-respecting professor of constitutional law.

Professor Corwin is spending his so-called "retirement" in Princeton, whence he goes forth from time to time to lecture to a new generation about the Constitution and its problems. Rather than rest contented with such honors as the presidency of the American Political Science Association (1931), a Litt. D. from Harvard (1936) and an LL.D. from both Michigan (1925) and Princeton (1954), and the Franklin medal of the American Philosophical Society (1940), he is toiling as faithfully and productively as ever in the lush vineyards of the American Constitution. The most recent fruits of this toil are *The Constitution and What It Means Today* (1954), the eleventh edition of a celebrated little book that first appeared in 1920, and *The Constitution of the United States of America: Analysis and Interpretation* (1953), an imposing public document of more than 1350 pages that serves each member of Congress as a trustworthy guide to the Constitution and to the more than 4000 cases that have made it what it is today.—*Clinton Rossiter.*

The "Higher Law" Background

of American Constitutional Law

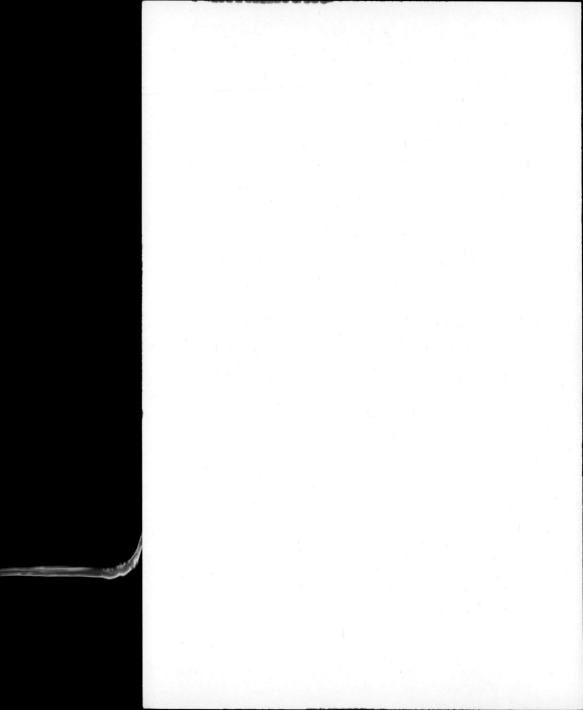

"Theory is the most important part of the dogma of the law, as the architect is the most important man who takes part in the building of a house." *

THE Reformation superseded an infallible Pope with an infallible Bible; the American Revolution replaced the sway of a king with that of a document. That such would be the outcome was not unforeseen from the first. In the same number of *Common Sense* which contained his electrifying proposal that America should declare her independence from Great Britain, Paine urged also a "Continental Conference," whose task he described as follows:

The conferring members being met, let their business be to frame a Continental Charter, or Charter of the United Colonies; (answering to what is called the Magna Charta of England) fixing the number and manner of choosing members of congress and members of assembly . . . and drawing the line of business and jurisdiction between them: (always remembering, that our strength is continental, not provincial) securing freedom and property to all men . . . with such other matter as it is necessary for a charter to contain. . . . But where, say some, is the King of America? Yet that we may not appear to be defective even in earthly honors, let a day be solemnly set apart for proclaiming the charter; let it be brought forth placed in the divine law, the word of God; let a crown be placed thereon, by which the world may

---

* HOLMES, COLLECTED LEGAL PAPERS (1921) 200.

know, that so far as we approve of monarchy, that in America the law is King.[1]

This suggestion, which was to eventuate more than a decade later in the Philadelphia Convention, is not less interesting for its retrospection than it is for its prophecy.

In the words of the younger Adams, "the Constitution itself had been extorted from the grinding necessity of a reluctant nation"; [2] yet hardly had it gone into operation than hostile criticism of its provisions not merely ceased but gave place to "an undiscriminating and almost blind worship of its principles" [3]—a worship which continued essentially unchallenged till the other day. Other creeds have waxed and waned, but "worship of the Constitution" has proceeded unabated.[4] It is true that the Abolitionists were accustomed to stigmatize the Constitution as "an agreement with Hell," but their shrill heresy only stirred the mass of Americans to renewed assertion of the national faith. Even Secession posed as loyalty to the *principles* of the Constitution and a protest against their violation, and in form at least the constitution of the Southern Confederacy was, with a few minor departures, a studied reproduction of the instrument of 1787. For by far the greater reach of its history, Bagehot's appraisal of the British monarchy is directly applicable to the Constitution: "The English Monarchy strengthens our government with the strength of religion." [5]

The fact that its adoption was followed by a wave of prosperity no doubt accounts for the initial launching of the Constitution upon the affections of the American people. Travelling through various parts of the United States at this time,

[1] 1 PAINE, POLITICAL WRITINGS (1837) 45–46.

[2] ADAMS, JUBILEE DISCOURSE ON THE CONSTITUTION (1839) 55.

[3] WOODROW WILSON, CONGRESSIONAL GOVERNMENT (13th ed. 1898) 4.

[4] On the whole subject, see 1 VON HOLST, CONSTITUTIONAL HISTORY (1877) c. 2; Schechter, *Early History of the Tradition of the Constitution* (1915) 9 AM. POL. SCI. REV. 707 *et seq.*

[5] BAGEHOT, ENGLISH CONSTITUTION (2d ed. 1925) 39. "The monarchy by its religious sanction now confirms all our political order. . . . It gives . . . a vast strength to the entire constitution, by enlisting on its behalf the credulous obedience of enormous masses." *Ibid.* 43–44.

2

Richard Bland Lee found "fields a few years ago waste and uncultivated filled with inhabitants and covered with harvests, new habitations reared, contentment in every face, plenty on every board. . . ." "To produce this effect," he continued, "was the intention of the Constitution, and it has succeeded." Indeed it is possible that rather too much praise was lavished upon the Constitution on this score. "It has been usual with declamatory gentlemen," complained the astringent Maclay, "in their praises of the present government, by way of contrast, to paint the state of the country under the old (Continental) congress, as if neither wood grew nor water ran in America before the happy adoption of the new Constitution;" and a few years later, when the European turmoil at once assisted, and by contrast advertised, our own blissful state, Josiah Quincy voiced a fear that "we have grown giddy with good fortune, attributing the greatness of our prosperity to our own wisdom, rather than to a course of events, and a guidance over which we had no influence." [6]

But while the belief that it drew prosperity in its wake may explain the beginning of the worship of the Constitution, it leaves a deeper question unanswered. It affords no explanation why this worship came to ascribe to the Constitution the precise virtues it did as an efficient cause of prosperity. To answer this question we must first of all project the Constitution against a background of doctrinal tradition which, widespread as European culture, was at the time of the founding of the English colonies especially strong in the mother country, though by the irony of history it had become a century and a half later the chief source of division between mother country and colonies.

It is customary nowadays to ascribe the *legality* as well as the *supremacy* of the Constitution—the one is, in truth, but the obverse of the other—exclusively to the fact that, in its own phraseology, it was "ordained" by "the people of the United States." Two ideas are thus brought into play. One is the so-called "positive" conception of law as a general expression

[6] Schechter, *supra* note 4, at 720–21.

merely for the particular commands of a human lawgiver, as a series of acts of human will; [7] the other is that the highest possible source of such commands, because the highest possible embodiment of human will, is "the people." The same two ideas occur in conjunction in the oft-quoted text of Justinian's *Institutes:* "Whatever has pleased the prince has the force of law, since the Roman people by the *lex regia* enacted concerning his *imperium,* have yielded up to him all their power and authority." [8] The sole difference between the Constitution of the United States and the imperial legislation justified in this famous text is that the former is assumed to have proceeded immediately from the people, while the latter proceeded from a like source only mediately.

The attribution of supremacy to the Constitution on the ground solely of its rootage in popular will represents, however, a comparatively late outgrowth of American constitutional theory. Earlier the supremacy accorded to constitutions was ascribed less to their putative source than to their supposed content, to their embodiment of an essential and unchanging justice. The theory of law thus invoked stands in direct contrast to the one just reviewed. *There are,* it is predicated, *certain principles of right and justice which are entitled to prevail of their own intrinsic excellence, altogether regardless of the attitude of those who wield the physical resources of the community.*

[7] Bentham, as quoted in HOLLAND, ELEMENTS OF JURISPRUDENCE (12th ed. 1916) 14. For further definitions of "positive law," see *ibid.* 22–23; WILLOUGHBY, FUNDAMENTAL CONCEPTS OF PUBLIC LAW (1924) c. 10.

[8] INST. I, 2, 6: "Quod principi placuit, legis habet vigorem, cum lege regia quae de ejus imperio lata est, populus ei et in eum, omne imperium suum et potestatem concessit." The source is ULPIAN, DIG. I, 4, 1. The Romans always regarded the people as the source of the legislative power. "Lex est, quod populus Romanus senatorie magistratu interrogante, veluti Consule, constituebat." INST. I, 2, 4. During the Middle Ages the question was much debated whether the *lex regia* effected an absolute alienation (*translatio*) of the legislative power to the Emperor, or was a revocable delegation (*cessio*). The champions of popular sovereignty at the end of this period, like Marsiglio of Padua in his *Defensor Pacis,* took the latter view. See GIERKE, POLITICAL THEORIES OF THE MIDDLE AGES (Maitland's tr. 1922) 150, notes 158, 159.

4

Such principles were made by no human hands; indeed, if they did not antedate deity itself, they still so express its nature as to bind and control it. They are external to all Will as such and interpenetrate all Reason as such. They are eternal and immutable. In relation to such principles, human laws are, when entitled to obedience save as to matters indifferent, merely a record or transcript, and their enactment an act not of will or power but one of discovery and declaration.[9] The Ninth Amendment of the Constitution of the United States, in stipulating that "the enumeration of certain rights in this Constitution shall not prejudice other rights not so enumerated," illustrates this theory perfectly except that the principles of transcendental justice have been here translated into terms of personal and private rights. The relation of such rights, nevertheless, to governmental power is the same as that of the principles from which they spring and which they reflect. They owe nothing to their recognition in the Constitution—such recognition was necessary if the Constitution was to be regarded as complete.

Thus the *legality* of the Constitution, its *supremacy,* and its claim to be worshipped, alike find common standing ground on the belief in a law superior to the will of human governors. Certain questions arise: Whence came this idea of a "higher law"? How has it been enabled to survive, and in what transformations? What special forms of it are of particular interest for the history of American constitutional law and theory? By what agencies and as a result of what causes was it brought to America and wrought into the American system of government? It is to these questions that the ensuing pages of this article are primarily addressed.

[I]

Words of Demosthenes attest the antiquity of the conception of law as a discovery: "Every law is a discovery, a gift of god,

[9] For definitions of law incorporating this point of view, see HOLLAND, *op. cit. supra* note 7, at 19–20, 32–36. *Cf.* 1 BL. COMM. Intro.

5

—a precept of wise men." [10] Words of President Coolidge prove the persistence of the notion: "Men do not make laws. They do but discover them. . . . That state is most fortunate in its form of government which has the aptest instruments for the discovery of law." [11] But not every pronouncement of even the most exalted human authority is necessarily law in this sense. This, too, was early asserted. A century before Demosthenes, Antigone's appeal against Creon's edict to the "unwritten and steadfast customs of the Gods" had already presented immemorial usage as superior to human rule-making.[12] A third stage in

[10] HOLLAND, *op. cit. supra* note 7, at 44n. "If there be any primitive theory of the nature of law, it seems to be that laws are the utterance of some divine or heroic person who reveals . . . that which is absolutely right." 1 POLLOCK AND MAITLAND, HISTORY OF ENGLISH LAW (1895) xxviii.

[11] COOLIDGE, HAVE FAITH IN MASSACHUSETTS (1919) 4. JOHN DICKINSON, ADMINISTRATIVE JUSTICE AND THE SUPREMACY OF LAW (1927), 85–86n., juxtaposes the above definitions, and also one from ST. AUGUSTINE, DE VERA RELIGIONE c. 31 in 34 MIGNE, PATROLOGIA LATINA (1845) 147: "Aeternam . . . legem mundis animis fas est congnoscere, judicare non fas est." This notion of the possibility of the spontaneous recognition of higher law has its counterpart in American constitutional theory, as will be pointed out later. Bacon voiced the "discovery" theory of law-making in the following words: "Regula enim legem (ut acus nautica polos) indicat, non statuit." DE JUSTITIA UNIVERSALI, Aphor. lxxxv, quoted in LORIMER, INSTITUTES OF LAW (2d ed. 1880) 256. Burke also accepted the theory: "It would be hard to point out any error more truly subversive of all the order and beauty, of all the peace and happiness of human society, than the position that any body of men have a right to make what laws they please; or that laws can derive any authority whatever from their institution merely, and independent of the quality of their subject-matter. . . . All human laws are, properly speaking, only declaratory. They may alter the mode and application, but have no power over the substance of original justice." BURKE, TRACT ON THE POPERY LAWS (c. 1780) c. 3, pt. 1, 6 BURKE, WORKS (1867) 322–23; LORIMER, *loc. cit. supra*. To the same effect is James Otis' assertion: "The supreme power in a state, is *jus dicere* only:—*jus dare*, strictly speaking, belongs only to God." OTIS, THE RIGHTS OF THE BRITISH COLONIES ASSERTED AND PROVED (1765) 70. For a brilliant effort to effect a logical reconciliation of the "positive" and the "discovery" theories of law making, in a modern terminology, see DEL VECCHIO, THE FORMAL BASES OF LAW (Mod. Leg. Philos. Ser. 1914).

[12] HOLLAND, *op. cit. supra* note 7, at 32n.; SOPHOCLES, ANTIGONE, vv, 450 *et seq.* Creon typifies in Sophocles' drama the Greek tyrant, whose coming had disturbed the ancient customary régime of the Greek city state.

the argument is marked by Aristotle's advice to advocates in his *Rhetoric* that, when they had "no case according to the law of the land," they should "appeal to the law of nature," and, quoting the Antigone of Sophocles, argue that "an unjust law is not a law." [13] The term law is, in other words, ambiguous. It may refer to a law of higher or a law of lower content; and, furthermore, some recourse should be available on the basis of the former against the latter.

But as Aristotle's own words show, the identification of higher law with custom did not remain the final word on the subject. Before this idea could enter upon its universal career as one of the really great humanizing forces of history, the early conception of it had to undergo a development not dissimilar to that of the Hebrew conception of God, although, thanks to the Sophists and to their critic, Socrates, the process was immensely abbreviated. The discovery that custom was neither immutable nor invariable even among the Greek city states impelled the Sophists to the conclusion that justice was either merely "the interest of the strong," or at best a convention entered upon by men purely on considerations of expediency and terminable on like considerations.[14] Ultimately, indeed, the two ideas boil down to the same thing, since it is impossible to regard as convenient that which cannot maintain itself, while that which can do so will in the long run be shaped to the interests of its sustainers. Fortunately these were not the only possible solutions to the problem posed by the Sophists. Building on Socrates' analysis of Sophistic teaching and Plato's theory of Ideas, Aristotle advanced in his *Ethics* the concept of "natural justice." "Of political justice," he wrote, "part is natural, part legal—natural, that which everywhere has the same force and does not exist by people's thinking this or that; legal, that

13 RITCHIE, NATURAL RIGHTS (1903) 30, citing ARISTOTLE, RHETORIC 1, 15, 1375, a, 27 *et seq.*

14 BARKER, THE POLITICAL THOUGHT OF PLATO AND ARISTOTLE (1906) 33–37. "Right is the interest of the stronger," says Thrasymachus in PLATO, REPUBLIC (Jowett tr. 1875) bk. I § 338. "Justice is a contract neither to do nor to suffer wrong," says Glaucon, *ibid.* bk. II, § 359. See also Philus in CICERO, DE REPUBLICA bk. III, 5.

which is originally indifferent. . . ." [15] That is to say, the essential ingredient of the justice which is enforced by the state is not of the state's own contrivance; it is a discovery from nature and a transcript of its constancy.

But practically what is the test of the presence of this ingredient in human laws and constitutions? By his conception of natural justice as universal, Aristotle is unavoidably led to identify the rational with the general in human laws. Putting the question in his *Politics* whether the rule of law or the rule of an individual is preferable, he answers his own inquiry in no uncertain terms. "To invest the law then with authority is, it seems, to invest God and reason only; to invest a man is to introduce a beast, as desire is something bestial, and even the best of men in authority are liable to be corrupted by passion. We may conclude then that the law is reason without passion and it is therefore preferable to any individual." [16] Nearly two thousand years after Aristotle, the sense of this passage, condensed into Harrington's famous phrase, "a government of laws and not of men," [17] was to find its way first into the Massachusetts constitution of 1780 [18] and then into Chief Justice Marshall's opinion in *Marbury v. Madison*.[19] The opposition which

[15] ARISTOTLE, NICOMECHEAN ETHICS (Ross tr. 1925) v, 7, §§ 1–2. See also BARKER, *op. cit. supra* note 14, at 328.

[16] ARISTOTLE, POLITICS (Welldon tr. 1905) bk. III, 15–16, especially at 154. I have departed slightly from the translation at one or two points. As Professor Barker points out, the Greek was apt to think of the law as an ideal code, the work of a sole legislator of almost superhuman wisdom, a Solon or a Lycurgus. Indeed, Plato and Aristotle look upon themselves as just such legislators. BARKER, *op. cit. supra* note 14, at 323. In comparison should be recalled the virtues attributed to the framers of the Constitution of the United States, and one source of its worship. On the equity of general laws enacted with deliberation and "without knowing on whom they were to operate," see Marshall, C. J., in *Ex parte* Bollman, 4 Cranch 75, 127 (U. S. 1807).

[17] HARRINGTON, OCEANA AND OTHER WORKS (1747) 37. "An empire of laws and not of men." *Ibid.* 45, 240; see also *ibid.* 49, 240, 257, 362, 369. Harrington ascribes the idea to Aristotle and Livy.

[18] DECLARATION OF RIGHTS, Art. 30; see THORPE, AMERICAN CHARTERS, CONSTITUTIONS, AND ORGANIC LAWS (1909).

[19] 1 Cranch 137, 163 (U. S. 1803).

it discovers between the desire of the human governor and the reason of the law lies, indeed, at the foundation of the American interpretation of the doctrine of the separation of powers and so of the entire American system of constitutional law.

It has been said of Plato that "he found philosophy a city of brick and left it a city of gold." [20] The operation of the Stoic philosophy upon the concept of a higher law may be characterized similarly. While Aristotle's "natural justice" was conceived primarily as a norm and guide for law makers, the *Jus Naturale* of the Stoics was the way of happiness for all men. The supreme legislator was Nature herself; nor was the natural order the merely material one which modern science exploits. The concept which Stoicism stressed was that of a moral order, wherein man through his divinely given capacity of reason was directly participant with the gods themselves. Nature, human nature, and reason were one.[21] The conception was, manifestly, an ethical, rather than a political or legal one, and for good cause. Stoicism arose on the ruins of the Greek city state. Plato's and Aristotle's belief that human felicity was to be achieved mainly by political means had proved illusory; and thrown back on his own resources, the Greek developed a new outlook, at once individualistic and cosmopolitan.

The restoration of the idea of natural law, enlarged and enriched by Stoicism, to the world's stock of legal and political ideas was accomplished by Cicero. In a passage of his *De Republica* which has descended to us through the writings of another (the preservative quality of a good style has rarely been so strikingly exemplified), Cicero sets forth his conception of natural law:

[20] JOUBERT, PENSÉES (5th ed. 1869) xxiv.

[21] On the doctrines of the Stoics, see DIOGENES LAERTIUS, LIVES AND OPINIONS OF EMINENT PHILOSOPHERS (Yonge tr. 1853) bk. vii, "Zeno," cc. 53, 55, 66, 70, 72–73. "Again, they say that justice exists by nature, and not because of any definition or principle; just as law does, or right reason." *Ibid.* c. 66. "The Stoics . . . thought of Nature or the Universe as a living organism, of which the material world was the body, and of which the Deity or the Universal Reason was the pervading, animating, and governing soul; and natural law was the rule of conduct laid down by this Universal Reason for the direction of mankind." SALMOND, JURISPRUDENCE (7th ed. 1924) 27.

True law is right reason, harmonious with nature, diffused among all, constant, eternal; a law which calls to duty by its commands and restrains from evil by its prohibitions. . . . It is a sacred obligation not to attempt to legislate in contradiction to this law; nor may it be derogated from nor abrogated. Indeed by neither the Senate nor the people can we be released from this law; nor does it require any but ourself to be its expositor or interpreter. Nor is it one law at Rome and another at Athens; one now and another at a late time; but one eternal and unchangeable law binding all nations through all time. . . .[22]

It is, however, in his *De Legibus* that Cicero makes his distinctive contribution. Identifying "right reason" with those qualities of human nature whereby "man is associated with the gods," [23] he there assigns the binding quality of the civil law itself to its being in harmony with such universal attributes of human nature. In the natural endowment of man, and especially his social traits, "is to be found the true source of laws and rights," [24] he asserts, and later says, "We are born for jus-

[22] LACTANTIUS, DIV. INST. (Roberts and Donaldson tr. 1871) vi, 8, 370; see also *ibid*. 24. It will be observed that Cicero does not overlook the imperative element of law. Bracton knew of the passage from the DE REPUBLICA, and Grotius' indebtedness to Cicero is beyond peradventure. "Jus naturale est dictatum rectae rationis. . . ." 1 GROTIUS, JURE BELLI AC PACIS (Whewell ed. 1853) 10. See also note 24, *infra*.

[23] CICERO, DE LEGIBUS (Müller ed.) I, 7, 23: "Inter quos autem ratio, inter eosdem etiam recta ratio et communis est; quae cum sit lex, lege quoque consociati homines cum dis putandi sumus." *Ibid*. I, 8, 25. "Est igitur homini cum deo similitudo." See also *ibid*. I, 7, 22-23. The entire passage is the source of Shakespeare's famous apostrophe to man in Hamlet. It ought to be remembered that the classical conception of "nature" was of an active, creative force, so that the "nature" of a thing became an innate tendency toward the realization of a certain ideal of the thing. Both Cicero's conception of "human nature" and his conception of "natural law" rest on this basis. The former is an expression of the highest attributes of man; the latter is the perfect expression of the idea of law.

[24] *Ibid*. I, 5, 16: "Nam sic habetote, nullo in genere disputando posse ita patefieri, quid sit homini a natura tributum, quantam vim rerum optimarum mens humana contineat, cujus muneris colendi efficiendique causa nati et in lucem editi simus, quae sit conjunctio hominum, quae naturalis societas inter ipsos; his enim explicatis fons legum et juris inveniri potest."

tice, and right is not the mere arbitrary construction of opinion, but an institution of nature." [25] Hence justice is not, as the Epicureans claim, mere utility, for "that which is established on account of utility may for utility's sake be overturned." [26] There is, in short, discoverable in the permanent elements of human nature itself a durable justice which transcends expediency, and the positive law must embody this if it is to claim the allegiance of the human conscience.

Ordinarily, moreover, human authority fulfills this requirement—this Cicero unquestionably holds. Hence his statement that "the laws are the foundation of the liberty which we enjoy; we all are the laws' slaves that we may be free." [27] The reference is clearly to the civil law. And of like import is his assertion that "nothing is more conformable to right and to the order of nature than authority [*imperium*]," [28] and the accompanying picture of the sway of law, in which the civil law becomes a part of the pattern of the entire fabric of universal order. That, none the less, the formal law, and especially enacted law, may at times part company with "true law" and thereby lose its title to be considered law at all, is, of course, implied by his entire position. We do have to rely upon implication. "Not all things," he writes, "are necessarily just which are established by the civil laws and institutions of nations"; nor is "justice identical with obedience to the written laws." [29] The vulgar, to be

---

This passage is especially significant for its emphasis upon certain qualities of human nature as the immediate source of natural law. The idea is not lacking in Stoic teaching, but it is subordinate. The same feature reappears in the continental natural law school of the seventeenth and eighteenth centuries. "Naturalis juris mater est ipsa humana natura," 1 GROTIUS, *op. cit. supra* note 22, Proleg. 16, xlix. Pufendorf and Burlamaqui also illustrate the same point of view, which contrasts with the legalism of Hobbes and Locke.

[25] CICERO, DE LEGIBUS I, 10, 28.   [26] *Ibid.* I, 15, 42.

[27] PRO A. CLUENTIO ORATIO c. 53, § 146.

[28] "Nihil porro tam aptum est ad jus condicionemque naturae . . . quam imperium, sine quo nec domus ulla nec civitas nec gens nec hominum universum genus stare nec rerum natura omnis nec ipse mundus potest. . . ." DE LEG. III, 1, 2–3.

[29] *Ibid.* I, 15, 42.

sure, are wont to apply the term "law" to whatever is "written, forbidding certain things and commanding others"; but it is so only in a colloquial sense.[30] "If it were possible to constitute right simply by the commands of the people, by the decrees of princes, by the adjudications of magistrates, then all that would be necessary in order to make robbery, adultery, or the falsification of wills right and just would be a vote of the multitude"; but "the nature of things" is not thus subject to "the opinions and behests of the foolish." [31] Despite which, "many pernicious and harmful measures are constantly enacted among peoples which do not deserve the name law." [32] True law is "a rule of distinction between right and wrong according to nature"; and "any other sort of law not only ought not to be regarded as law, it ought not to be called law." [33]

But what, when that which wears the form of law is at variance with true law, is the remedy? Certain Roman procedural forms connected with the enactment of law suggested to Cicero, in answering this question, something strikingly like judicial review. It was a Roman practice to incorporate in statutes a saving clause to the effect that it was no purpose of the enactment to abrogate what was sacrosanct or *jus*.[34] In this way certain

---

[30] *Ibid.* I, 6, 19. [31] *Ibid.* I, 16, 43–44. [32] *Ibid.* II, 5, 13.
[33] *Ibid.* II, 6, 13.

[34] See Brissonius (Barnabé Brisson), De Formulis et Solennibus Populi Romani Verbis (Leipsic, 1754) Lib. 2, c. 19, 129–30. This admirable work first appeared in 1583. The Leipsic edition, for the loan of which I have to thank the authorities of the Elbert H. Gary Library of Law, is based on a revision and extension of the original work by one Franciscus Conradus, and contains a life of Brisson, who was one time President of the Parlement of Paris. The customary form of the saving clause was, "Si quid sacri sanctique est, quod jus non sit rogari, ejus hac lege nihil rogatur." In his Pro Caecina Oratio, Cicero gives a somewhat different form, taken from an enactment of Sulla: "Si quid jus non esset rogari, ejus ea lege nihilum rogatum," *Ibid.* cc. 32–33. A variant on this form appears in his Pro Domo Sua c. 40. See note 37, *infra*. On these occasions Cicero is relying on the saving clause; but in his Pro Balbo, the shoe is on the other foot, and he there argues against the extension of such a clause to a certain treaty, that nothing can be "sacrosanctum—nisi quod populus plebesve sanxisset," whereas the treaty in question had been made by the Senate. *Ibid.* c. 14.

maxims, or *leges legum,* as Cicero styles them,[35] some of which governed the legislative process itself,[36] were erected into a species of written constitution binding on the legislative power. More than once we find Cicero, in reliance on such a clause, invoking *jus* against a statute. "What is it," he inquires on one such occasion, "that is not *jus!* . . . This saving clause [*adscriptio*] declares that it is something, otherwise it would not be provided against in all our laws. And I ask you, if the people had commanded that I should be your slave, or you mine, would that be validly enacted, fixed, established?" [37] On other occasions he points out that it was within the power both of the Augurs and of the Senate to abrogate laws which had not been enacted *jure,* though here the reference may be to the procedure of legislation, and he mentions instances of the exercise of these purgative powers.[38] And on one occasion, in addressing the Senate, we find him appealing directly to *"recta ratio"* as against the *"lex scripta."* [39]

Whether Cicero's adumbrations of judicial review ever actually came to the attention of the framers of the American constitutional system to any considerable extent seems ex-

---

Cicero himself suffered from "a new and previously unheard of use" of the clause by his enemy Clodius, who endeavored by affixing it to the law exiling Cicero and confiscating his property, to render the latter irrepealable. For Cicero's argument against the possibility of thus clothing statutes with immortality, see EPISTOLAE, III, 22; BRISSONIUS, *supra,* at 130.

[35] CICERO, DE LEGIBUS II, 7, 18. Here Cicero is dealing with the laws of religion. In book three he treats of the civil laws similarly.

[36] "The *lex Caecilia et Didia* was a portion of the *jus legum* which prohibited the proposal of any law containing two or more matters not germane." COXE, JUDICIAL POWER AND UNCONSTITUTIONAL LEGISLATION (1893) iii, citing SMITH, DICTIONARY OF GREEK AND ROMAN ANTIQUITIES (1842) art. *lex.*

[37] PRO CAECINA c. 33. *Cf.* PRO DOMO SUA c. 40. I must acknowledge the valuable assistance so kindly lent by my friend, Professor John Dickinson, in tracing down these anticipations by Cicero of judicial review.

[38] CICERO, DE LEGIBUS II, 12, 31; PRO DOMO SUA cc. 16, 26, 27.

[39] PHIL. XI, 12. Here Cicero invokes natural law in the public interest— an anticipation of one aspect of the doctrine of the police power.

tremely doubtful.[40] Taken, none the less, along with Aristotle's similar suggestion, they serve to show how immediate, if not inevitable, is the step from the notion of a higher law entering into the civil law to that of a regular recourse against the latter on the basis of the former. And if Cicero did not contribute to the establishment of judicial review directly, he at any rate did so indirectly through certain ideas of his which enter into the argumentative justification of that institution. The first of these is his assertion that natural law requires no interpreter other than the individual himself,[41] a notion which is still sometimes reflected in the contention of courts and commentators that unconstitutional statutes are unconstitutional *per se,* and not because of any authority attaching to the court that so pronounces them. The other consists in his description of the magistrate as "the law speaking [*magistratum legem esse loquentem, legem autem mutum magistratum*]." [42] The sense of this passage from the *De Legibus* is reproduced in Coke's *Reports* in the words, *"Judex est lex loquens."* [43] The importance of both these ideas for the doctrine of judicial review will be indicated later.

Of the other features of the Ciceronian version of natural

[40] There is, however, one apparent instance of this happening. In the notes for his argument in Rutgers v. Waddington, Mayor's Ct., New York City (1784), Hamilton included the following passage: "Si leges duae aut si plures aut quot quot erunt conservari non possunt quia discrepent inter se ea maxime conservanda sunt quae ad maximas res pertinere videatur," citing De In: L 4, No. 145. See A. M. HAMILTON, HAMILTON (1910) 462. The passage is in fact from DE INVENTIONE II, 49. The context casts some doubt on whether it was intended by Cicero in quite the sense for which Hamilton appears to have employed it.

[41] "Neque est quarendus explanator, aut interpres ejus alius." DE REP. III, 22; LACTANTIUS, DIV. INST. vi, 8. See also note 11, *supra.*

[42] CICERO, DE LEGIBUS III, 1, 2–3.

[43] Calvin's Case, 4 Co. 1 (1609). "Neither have Judges power to judge according to that which they think to be fit, but that which out of the laws they know to be right and consonant to law. *Judex bonus nihil ex arbitrio suo faciat, nec proposito domesticae voluntatis, sed juxta leges et jura pronuntiet." Ibid.* 27(a). See Chief Marshall's rendition of the same idea in Osborn v. Bank of United States, 9 Wheat. 738, 866 (U. S. 1824): "Judicial power, as contradistinguished from the power of the laws, has no existence." The maxim which assigns to the judges the power of *jus dicere* but not

law, the outstanding one is his conception of human equality:

> There is no one thing so like or so equal to one another as in every instance man is to man. And if the corruption of custom and the variation of opinion did not induce an imbecility of minds and turn them aside from the course of nature, no one would more resemble himself than all men would resemble all men. Therefore, whatever definition we give to man will be applicable to the entire human race.[44]

Not only is this good Stoic teaching, it is the inescapable consequence of Cicero's notion of the constancy of the distinctive attributes of human nature, those which supply the foundation of natural law.

With respect to certain other elements of the doctrine of natural law as it entered American constitutional theory, the allocation of credit cannot be made so confidently. The notion of popular sovereignty,[45] of a social contract,[46] and of contract between governors and governed [47] are all foreshadowed by Cicero with greater or less distinctness. The notion of a state of nature, on the other hand, is missing, being supplied by Seneca

---

that of *jus dare* is traceable to BACON, ESSAYS, *Judicature* (Reynolds' ed. 1890) 365. On the entire subject see my article, *The Progress of Constitutional Theory, 1776–1787* (1924–25) 30 AM. HIST. REV. 511–36; see also notes 104 and 121, *infra*.

[44] CICERO, DE LEGIBUS I, 10, 12–28, 33. "There is no conception which is more fundamental to the Aristotelian theory of society than the notion of the natural inequality of human nature. . . . There is no change in political theory so startling in its completeness as the change from the theory of Aristotle to the later philosophical view represented by Cicero and Seneca. Over against Aristotle's view of the natural inequality of human nature we find set the theory of the natural equality of human nature. . . . There is only one possible definition for all mankind, reason is common to all." 1 CARLYLE, A HISTORY OF MEDIAEVAL POLITICAL THEORY (1927) 7–8. The identification of *jus naturale* with *recta ratio,* the universal possession of mankind, leads to the doctrine of the equality of mankind, and this in turn paves the way for the translation of *natural law* into *natural rights*.

[45] DE REP. I, 25. Editors also assign to the same chapter, preserved by St. Augustine, the following: "Quid est res publica nisi res populi? Res ergo communis, res utique civitatis." See ST. AUGUSTINE, EPISTLES 138, 10, and DE CIVITATE DEI v, 18. From what has been said already, it is evident that the notion of popular sovereignty cannot be attributed to Cicero in the sense of unlimited legislative power. See DE REP. III, 3. See notes 8 and 37, *supra*.

and the early Church Fathers, the latter locating their primitive polity in the Garden of Eden before the Fall.[48] It is Seneca also who corrects Cicero's obtuseness, later repeated by the signers of the Declaration of Independence, to the contradiction between the idea of equality of man and the institution of slavery; [49] and his views were subsequently ratified by certain of the great Roman jurists. Ulpian, writing at the close of the second century, asserts unqualifiedly that "by the law of nature all men are born free," words which are repeated in the *Institutes* three hundred years later.[50] Natural law is already putting forth the stem of natural rights that is ultimately to dwarf and overshadow it.

The eloquence of Cicero's championship of *jus naturale* was

[46] DE REP. I, 26, 32; *ibid.* III, 31. "Generale quippe pactum est societatis humanae oboedire regibus." ST. AUGUSTINE, CONFESSIONS (Gibb & Montgomery tr. 1908) III, 8. "Est autem civitas coetus perfectus liberorum hominum juris fruendi et communis utilitatis causa sociatus." 1 GROTIUS, *op. cit. supra* note 22, at I, 14. It should be recalled that *societas* in Roman private law meant partnership. The idea of the *civitas* as a deliberately formed association smacks of Epicurean and Sophistic ideas, rather than Stoic, but there is no necessary conflict between it and Stoic conceptions. That which is done with deliberation may still be done in response to natural impulse and necessity. The contribution of the Middle Ages to the social contract theory sprang from the nature of feudal society, and was a deepened sense of the obligation of contracts. See GIERKE, POLITICAL THEORIES OF THE MIDDLE AGES (Maitland tr. 1922) notes 303, 306, and GIERKE, ALTHUSIUS (Zur deutschen Staats u. Rechts Geschichte 1879–80) 99 *et seq.;* also note 61, *infra.*

[47] DE REP. III, 13. This is an interesting forecast of the process of "commendation" by which feudalism actually did arise in parts of Europe.

[48] 1 CARLYLE, *op. cit. supra* note 44, at 23–25, 117, 134, 144–46; GIERKE, ALTHUSIUS 92–94; LANCTANTIUS, DIV. INST. v, 5. *Cf.* LUCRETIUS, DE RERUM NATURA (Merrill ed. 1907) v, 11, 1105–60. Especially to be noted is Lucretius' phrase, "communia foedera pacis." *Ibid.* at 1155.

[49] 1 CARLYLE, *op. cit. supra* note 44. Aristotle in his POLITICS is evidently dealing with an attack on slavery. ARISTOTLE, POLITICS i, 4–7. A certain Alcidamos is reported to have said (4th century?): "God made all men free; nature made none a slave." RITCHIE, NATURAL RIGHTS (1903) 25.

[50] DIG. I, 1, 4; INST. I, 2, 2. Slavery is explained by Ulpian by reference to the *jus gentium.* "Quod ad jus naturale attinet, omnes aequales sunt." DIG. L, 17, 32; see 1 CARLYLE, *op. cit. supra* note 44, at 47.

matched by its timeliness. It brought the Stoic conception of a universal law into contact with Roman law at the moment when the administrators of the latter were becoming aware of the problem of adapting a rigid and antique code, burdened with tribal ceremoniousness and idiosyncrasy, to the needs of an empire which already overshadowed the Mediterranean world. In the efforts of the *praetor peregrinus* to meet the necessities of foreigners resorting to Rome, a beginning had early been made toward the building up of a code which, albeit without the conscious design of its authors, approximated in many ways to the Stoic ideal of simplicity and of correspondence with the fundamental characteristics of human relationship; but the clear presentation of the Stoic ideal to the Roman jurists may be imagined to have stimulated this development vastly. The outcome is to be seen in the concept of *jus gentium,* which is defined by Gaius and later in the *Institutes,* as "that law which natural reason established among all mankind" and "is observed equally by all peoples," whereas the *jus civile* of each people is peculiar to itself.[51] Recast in the light of this conception the Roman civil law became the universal code, and by the same token *jus naturale* took on the semblance of a law with definite content and guaranteed enforcement—in a word, that of "positive law." [52]

The conception of a higher law pervades the Middle Ages; it also becomes sharpened to that of a code distinctively for rulers. In the pages of the *Policraticus* of the Englishman, John of Salisbury, the first systematic writer on politics in the Middle Ages, one learns that "there are certain precepts of the law which have perpetual necessity, having the force of law

[51] INST. I, 2, 1–2. Gaius, in contrast with Ulpian, regards the *jus gentium* as identical with *jus naturale.* 1 CARLYLE, *op. cit. supra* note 44, at 38; BRYCE, STUDIES IN HISTORY AND JURISPRUDENCE (1901) 581.

[52] This work of revision fell to the great jurisconsults. As Dean Pound has pointed out: "The jurisconsult had no legislative power and no *imperium.* The authority of his *responsum* . . . was to be found in its intrinsic reasonableness; in the appeal which it made to the reason and sense of justice of the *judex* . . . it was law by nature. POUND, INTRODUCTION TO THE PHILOSOPHY OF LAW (1922) 29.

among all nations and which absolutely cannot be broken." [53] This clear reflection of the Ciceronian conception of natural law had found its way to later centuries notably through the writings of Saint Isidore of Seville and the *Decretum* of Gratian.[54] But joined with the same conception, and clearly contributing to its survival over a critical period, was the identification of the higher law with Scripture, with the teachings of the Church, and with the *Corpus Juris*. As remarked by his translator, John was not confronted with the difficulty which has so often troubled later exponents of *jus naturale* "of identifying any specific rules or precepts as belonging to this law." He had them "in the form of clear cut scripture texts" and in maxims of the Roman law.[55]

Of even greater importance is the fact that John addresses his counsels exclusively to princes. There were two sets of reasons for this. On the one hand, yielding to the Christian dispensation with its "other world" outlook, *jus naturale* had lost all significance as a "way of life" the promised goal of which was earthly bliss. At the same time, the art of legislation, which Aristotle and Cicero always had pre-eminently in mind, had for the time being ceased to exist. On the other hand was the Teutonic conception of the ruler as simply soldier and judge. The business of the judge, however, is justice; yet justice by what standard? The answer that John returns to this question is in effect *jus naturale* furnished out with the content just described.

A not less significant feature of John's doctrine is his insistence upon the distinction between "a tyrant" as "one who op-

[53] DICKINSON, THE STATESMAN'S BOOK OF JOHN OF SALISBURY (1927) 33.

[54] POLLOCK, ESSAYS IN THE LAW (1922) 40 *es seq.;* 2 CARLYLE, *op. cit. supra* note 44, at 29, 41, 94–109. Gratian discusses the question why it was that while the *jus naturale* is contained in the "law," some of the latter is variable. He concludes that not all law is natural law, even when it claims the support of God. *Ibid.* 109. Later medieval writers distinguish two varieties of the *jus naturale,* the higher and the lower, of which only the first is unchangeable. Gratian also passes on to us the phrase *jus constitutionis,* signifying a system of written law, the first example being the legislation of Moses. *Ibid.* 115.

[55] DICKINSON, *op. cit. supra* note 53, at xxxv.

presses the people by rulership based upon force" and "a prince" as "one who rules in accordance with the laws." [56] In these words John foreshadows the distinctive contribution of the Middle Ages to modern political science—the notion of all political authority as intrinsically limited. Proceeding from this point of view, John makes short work of those troublesome texts of Roman law which assert that the prince is *"legibus solutus"* [57] and that "what he has willed has the force of law." [58] It is not true, he answers, that the prince is absolved from the obligations of the law "in the sense that it is lawful for him to do unjust acts," but only in the sense that his character should guarantee his doing equity "not through fear of the penalties of the law but through love of justice"; and as to "the will of the prince," in respect of public matters, "he may not lawfully have any will of his own apart from that which the law or equity enjoins, or the calculation of the common interest requires." [59] Indeed the very title *rex* is derived from doing right, that is, acting in accordance with law *(recte)*.[60]

The sweep and majesty of the medieval conception of a higher law as at once the basis and test for all rightful power is emphasized by the German historian, von Gierke. Natural law constrained the highest earthly powers. It held sway over Pope and Emperor, over ruler and sovereign people alike, indeed over the whole community of mortals. Neither statute *(Gesetz)* nor any act of authority, neither usage nor popular

[56] *Ibid.* 335. The notion that the prince is subject to the law is, of course, much older than the *Policraticus*. Stobaeus credits Solon with saying that "that was the best government where the subjects obeyed their prince, and the prince the laws." Notice also Fortescue's quotation from Diodorus Siculus, that "the kings of Egypt originally did not live in such a licentious manner as other kings, whose will was their law: but were subject to the same law, in common with the subject, and esteemed themselves happy in such a conformity to the laws." FORTESCUE, DE LAUDIBUS LEGUM ANGLIAE (Amos tr. 1825) c. XIII.

[57] DIG. I, 3, 31.   [58] See note 8, *supra.*

[59] DICKINSON, *op. cit. supra* note 53, at 7.

[60] *Ibid.* 336. See also *ibid.* lxvii–iii, notes 221–22, and ZANE, STORY OF LAW (1927) 214.

resolve could break through the limits which it imposed. Anything which conflicted with its eternal and indestructible principles was null and void and could bind nobody. Furthermore, while there was no sharp disseverance of natural law from morality, yet the limits thrown about the legitimate sphere of supreme power should by no means, von Gierke insists, be regarded as merely ethical principles. Not only were they designed to control external acts and not merely the ruler's internal freedom, but they were addressed also to judges and to all having anything to do with the application of the law, who were thereby bound to hold for naught not only any act of authority but even any statute which overstepped them. They morally exonerated the humblest citizen in defiance of the highest authority; they might even justify assassination.[61]

Read in the light of Austinian conceptions, these words may easily convey a somewhat exaggerated impression. Yet the outstanding fact is clear that the supposed precepts of a higher law were, throughout the Middle Ages, being continually pitted against the claims of official authority and were being continually set to test the validity of such claims. At the same time was occurring throughout Western Europe the ever renewed contest between secular and ecclesiastical authority over the question of jurisdiction. The total result was to bring the conception of all authority as inherently conditional to a high pitch of expression.

Furthermore, the Middle Ages—which is to say certain

---

[61] GIERKE, *op. cit. supra* note 46, at 75–76, 85; GIERKE, ALTHUSIUS 272, and n.22, where Aquinas, Occam, Baldus, Alliacus, Cusanus, Gerson, and others are cited; *ibid.* 275–76 and notes 30 and 31. The doctrine was stated that when the Emperor acted against the law he did not act as emperor ("non facit ut imperator"). Bartolus and his followers attributed greater authority to statutes than to judicial judgments, but held none the less that even statutes contrary to natural law were void. Laws were binding, it was taught, so far as they concerned those matters "quae ad potestatem pertinent, non in iis quae ad tyrranidem"; nor was a superior entitled to obedience "quando egriditur fines sui officii." See also *ibid.* 142, n.57, where Occam is cited for the expression "potestas limitata." See also 2 CARLYLE, *op. cit. supra* note 44, at 32, 78, 79.

writers of that period—must also be credited with at least a partial apprehension of the concept of natural rights. This is to be seen in the reference to *jus gentium* of the two most fundamental of modern legal institutions, private property and contracts. In the words of von Gierke: "Property had its roots . . . in Law which flowed out of the pure Law of Nature without the aid of the State and in Law which was when as yet the State was not. Thence it followed that particular rights which had been acquired by virtue of this Institution in no wise owed their existence exclusively to the State." Likewise, the binding force of contracts was traced from natural law, "so that the Sovereign, though he could not bind himself or his successors by Statute, could bind himself and his successors by Contract." It followed thence "that every right which the State had conferred by way of Contract was unassailable by the State," exception alone being made in the case of "interferences proceeding *ex justa causa*." [62]

In the writings which von Gierke thus summarizes, notably

[62] Gierke, *op. cit. supra* note 46, at 80–81, and notes 278, 279. To same effect is Gierke, Althusius 270–71, and notes 18 and 19. "Deus ipse ex promissione obligatur," wrote Decius Constantinus. Writers of the Middle Ages, it might be explained, distinguished *jus naturale, jus divinum,* and *jus gentium.* The first was described as having been planted by God in natural reason for purely mundane ends; the second as having been communicated by a supernatural revelation for purely supramundane ends, the last as those rules which flowed from the pure *jus naturale* when due account was taken of the human relationships which resulted from the fall of man, of which property and contract were instances. *Jus gentium* thus tended to take on a certain appearance of positive law, while the broader concept tended to be relegated to the sphere of ethics, lying midway between law proper and religion. Thus despite von Gierke's sweeping statement, which is substantially correct for the civilians, there would seem to have been considerable conflict of opinion among the canonists, deriving from the communism of the Church Fathers, whether property existed even mediately by *jus naturale.* 2 Carlyle, *op. cit. supra* note 44, at 49 *et seq.* St. Germain, Doctor and Student, written early in the sixteenth century, reflects this doubt. See the *Second Dialogue* in Doctor and Student (Muchall ed. 1787) 99. Von Gierke also asserts that "Mediaeval Doctrine was already filled with the thought of the inborn and indestructible rights of the Individual, the formulation and classification" of

those of the Glossators and their successors, the emphasis, it is true, is upon the sanctity of the two institutions of property and contract as such. Yet both of these are quickly resolvable into terms of individual interest. The strong initial bias of American constitutional law in favor of rights of property and contract has, therefore, its background in speculations of the Middle Ages.

Upon the observed uniformities of the human lot, classical antiquity erected the conception of a law of nature discoverable by human reason when uninfluenced by passion, and forming the ultimate source and explanation of the excellence of positive law. *Jus naturale* was thus a code which challenged the skill and stirred the intuition of legislators, and in the *Corpus Juris* the triumph of Roman jurisprudence in its approximation to this noble goal is to be seen. The inauguration of the Middle Ages was marked by the reverse process. An almost complete paralysis of legislative activity characterized the outset of this period, and as this fact indicates, rulership had become personal, irresponsible, and unhampered by institutional control. Meeting the needs of the time, a new attitude toward higher law became predominant. Definite texts of Roman law, teachings of the Church, and scriptural passages were projected upward, to become a mystic overlaw, "a brooding omnipresence in the sky." [63] The purpose of this naïve construction, the very reverse of that which generally pervades antique conceptions, was not to account for a prevalent justice but rather to correct a prevalent injustice, not to enlighten authority but rather to circumscribe it. In other words, whereas the classical conception of natural law was that it conferred its chief benefits by enter-

---

which, he admits, "belonged to a later stage in the growth of the theory of Natural Law." This and his sharp contrast between "the theories of Antiquity" and the "thought revealed by Christianity and grasped in all its profundity by the Germanic Spirit" bespeak perhaps the enthusiastic Teutonist rather than the critical historian. GIERKE, POLITICAL THEORIES OF THE MIDDLE AGES 81–82; GIERKE, ALTHUSIUS 274–75.

[63] Compare Mr. Justice Holmes in Southern Pac. Ry. v. Jensen, 244 U. S. 205, 222 (1917).

ing into the more deliberate acts of human authority, the medieval conception was that it checked and delimited authority from without.[64] This conception, the direct inheritance of American constitutional theory from the Middle Ages, was confirmed by the current struggle between Papacy and Empire over the question of jurisdiction, as it has been confirmed in American constitutional theory by the existence of a similar issue between the nation and the states.

That, on the other hand, the practical importance of the higher law doctrine in actually frustrating political injustice during this era may be easily exaggerated is, so far as the Continent is concerned, clearly apparent. Lacking the institutional equipment to make good its claims except very haphazardly, lacking, too, a final authoritative interpretation except at times that of the Papacy, the conception still remained, after all the confident asseverations of generations of writers, relatively vague and ineffective, and altogether incapable, as time revealed, of repelling despotism once the latter was furnished with an answering argument, as it was from the beginning of the sixteenth century. In England alone were these deficiences supplied in appreciable measure, and in England alone were the pretensions of divine right defeated in the following century. So while we look to the Continent during the Middle Ages for ideas, we look to England during the same period for both ideas and institutions.

[II]

The eve of the controversy over rights which preceded the American Revolution found John Adams, a briefless attorney of twenty-eight, paying the following tribute to the subject of his favorite studies:

[64] In ancient theory *jus naturale* was a *terminus ad quem*—a goal toward which actual law inevitably tended; in medieval theory it was a *terminus a quo*—a standard from which human authority was always straying. Cicero's optimism regarding human nature offers a similar and not unrelated contrast to the Christian doctrine of original sin.

It has been my amusement for many years past, as far as I have had leisure, to examine the systems of all the legislators, ancient and modern, fantastical and real . . . , and the result . . . is a settled opinion that the liberty, the unalienable, indefeasible rights of men, the honor and dignity of human nature, the grandeur and glory of the public, and the universal happiness of individuals, were never so skillfully and successfully consulted as in that most excellent monument of human art, the common law of England.[65]

This passage conveys admirably the outstanding characteristic of English higher law. Before it was higher law it was positive law in the strictest sense of the term, a law regularly administered in the ordinary courts in the settlement of controversies between private individuals. Many of the rights which the Constitution of the United States protects at this moment against legislative power were first protected by the common law against one's neighbors. The problem we have hitherto been discussing takes on consequently an altered emphasis as we approach higher law concepts in medieval England. The question is no longer how certain principles that ought to be restrictive of political authority took on a legal character or of the extent to which they did so, but rather how certain principles of a legal character in their origin assumed the further quality of principles entitled to control authority and to control it as law. In other words, the problem is not how the common law became *law*, but how it became *higher*, without at the same time ceasing to be enforceable through the ordinary courts even within the field of its more exalted jurisdiction.

The generation in which the Constitution was framed was wont to ascribe the transcendental quality of the common law above all to its vast antiquity.[66] Nor was this by any means the

---

[65] ADAMS, LIFE AND WORKS (1851) 440; and see note 96, *infra*.

[66] "Alfred . . . magnus juris Anglicani conditor . . . with the advice of his wise men, collected out of the laws of Ina, Offa, and Ethelbert such as were best, and made them to extend equally to the whole nation." Later kings, Edward the Elder, Edward the Confessor, William the Conqueror, and so on, continued the good work. "King John swore to restore them [the laws]; King Henry III confirmed them; Magna Charta was founded on them, and King Edward I in parliament, confirmed them." 3 ADAMS, LIFE

first appearance of the idea. The Conqueror professed to restore the laws of Edward the Confessor, and Stephen did the same in the century following. The idea was, obviously, a politically valuable one, since it proclaimed from the first the existence of a body of law owing nothing to royal authority and capable therefore of setting limits to that authority. That the substance of the common law as it was known in 1787 really antedated the Norman Conquest is, none the less, the veriest fiction, however important a one. As Sir Frederick Pollock has observed: "For most practical purposes the history of English law does not begin till after the Norman Conquest, and the earliest things which modern lawyers are strictly bound to know must be allowed to date only from the thirteenth century, and from the latter half of it rather than the former." [67] Indeed the so-called dooms which the constitutional fathers were wont to regard so worshipfully were, by modern standards, pretty poor affairs, being filled in large part "by minute catalogues of the fines and compositions payable for manslaughter, wounding, and other acts of violence"; while the most important of them in legend, the laws of Edward the Confessor, were, in the form in which they have come down to us, an antiquarian compilation in verse dating from the twelfth century.[68]

The true starting point in the history of the common law is the establishment by Henry II in the third quarter of the twelfth century of a system of circuit courts with a central appeal court. To this fact beyond all others is due one striking difference between English and Continental higher law. The

---

AND WORKS 541–42. To like effect was Jefferson's quaint theory that the American constitutional system only restored to mankind the long lost polity of Anglo-Saxon England, along with which was broached the notion that the Tories of eighteenth century England were the lineal descendants of the Normans and the Whigs the Saxons. *Jefferson to Cartwright, June 5, 1824*, in 7 JEFFERSON, WRITINGS (Washington ed. 1854) 355; JEFFERSON, COMMON PLACE BOOK (Chinard ed. 1926) 351–62.

[67] 1 SELECT ESSAYS IN ANGLO-AMERICAN LEGAL HISTORY (1907) 88.

[68] *Ibid.* 97. See also *English Law Before the Norman Conquest* in POLLOCK, EXPANSION OF THE COMMON LAW (1904) 139.

latter was not regarded as incorporating indigenous custom—rather it was an appeal from it—for the reason that on the Continental custom remained till the French Revolution purely local. The common law, on the contrary, was regarded from the first as based upon custom. In truth it was custom gradually rendered national, that is to say, common, through the judicial system just described. Yet it was not custom alone. For in their selection of what customs to recognize in order to give them national sway, and what to suppress, the judges employed the test of "reasonableness," [69] a test derived in the first instance from Roman and Continental ideas. Indeed, the notion that the common law embodied right reason furnished from the fourteenth century its chief claim to be regarded as higher law. But once again a sharp divergence must be noted from Continental ideas. The right reason to which the maxims of higher law on the Continent were addressed was always the right reason invoked by Cicero, it was the right reason of all men. The right reason which lies at the basis of the common law, on the other hand, was from the beginning *judicial* right reason. Considered as an act of knowledge or discovery, the common law was the act of experts, and increasingly so, with the ever firmer establishment of the doctrine of *stare decisis*.

With certain nineteenth century historians of the law in mind, Dean Pound voices the legitimate complaint that they will not "hear of an element of creative activity of men as lawyers, judges, writers of books, or legislators. . . . They think of the phenomena of legal development as events, as if men were not acting in the bringing about of every one of them. For the so-called events of legal history are in truth acts of definite men, or even of a definite man." [70] Certainly the history of the common law is far from being a mere anonymous tradition; and especially is this so of the story of its elevation to the position of a higher law binding upon supreme authority. The story of *Magna Carta* is an important chapter in this larger

[69] For illustrative cases see ALLEN, LAW IN THE MAKING (1927) 359 *et seq.* *Cf.* Co. INST. I, 113(a).

[70] POUND, INTERPRETATIONS OF LEGAL HISTORY (1923) 118.

story, and for our purposes is sufficiently treated as an event. But it is otherwise with the labors of that series of judicial commentators on the common law which begins with Bracton and ends with Blackstone. The signal contribution of each to the final result still remains identifiable—their total contribution spans some five hundred years.

Bracton, Henry of Bratton, was a judge of the King's Bench in the reign of Henry III.[71] His great work, in preparation for which, in addition to his studies of Roman law, he collected some two thousand decisions, is entitled *De Legibus et Consuetudinibus Angliae.* For us the outstanding importance of the work consists in the fact that for the first time it brought the rising common law into direct contact with Roman and medieval Continental ideas of a higher law. "The King himself," runs an oft-quoted passage of this treatise, "ought not to be subject to man, but subject to God and to the law, for the law makes the King. Let the King then attribute to the law what the law attributes to him, namely, dominion and power, for there is no King where the will and not the law has dominion." [72] In these words we have again the characteristic medieval idea of all authority as deriving from the law and as, therefore, limited by it. Bracton's own words, it will be noted, are strongly reminiscent of John of Salisbury, and elsewhere the similarity becomes even more striking. The King's power, he writes, is the power of justice, not of injustice. So long as he does justice, the King is the vicar of God; but when he turns aside to injustice, he is the minister of the devil. Indeed, he is called King (*rex*) from ruling well (*regendo*), not from reigning (*regnando*). "Let him therefore, temper his power by law, which is the bridle of power . . . likewise is nothing so appropriate to empire as to live according to the laws, and to submit the princedom to law is greater than empire." [73]

[71] For an excellent sketch of Bracton's life see the *Introduction* in 1 BRACTON, NOTE BOOK (Maitland's tr. 1887) 13–25.

[72] BRACTON, DE LEGIBUS ET CONSUETUDINIBUS ANGLIAE (Twiss ed. 1854) f. 5b.

[73] *Ibid.* f. 107b. *Cf.* DICKINSON, *op. cit. supra* note 53, at lxviii, cc. 1, 2, 17, 22.

What sharply distinguishes Bracton from his predecessors and contemporaries—men like John of Salisbury and Saint Thomas Aquinas—is his conception of law. Thanks to his study of the Roman law, and even more perhaps to his experience as judge, this is even by modern tests strikingly positivistic. He lets us know at the outset that the law (*lex*) which he has primarily in mind is the law which rests on "the common sanction of the body politic." It embraces various elements: customs (unwritten laws), decisions of prudent men, which in like cases should be treated as precedents—"It is good occasion to proceed from like to like"—and finally the law made by the King in Council.[74] The question arises whether he considered the last category as subject to any limitation, and on this point Bracton is ambiguous. Discussing the maxim that "the pleasure of the prince has the force of law," he says that it applies not to "whatever is rashly presumed of the King's own will" but only to "that which has been rightly defined with the counsel of his magistrates, the King himself authorising it, and deliberation and discussion having been had upon it."[75] The implication is that the requirements mentioned having been met in its expression, the will of the prince does have the force of law. And not less noteworthy is his attitude toward *jura naturalia;* these are said to be immutable because they cannot be repealed in their entirety; but in fact they can be and have been abrogated in part. Yet at the same time he asserts, in words harking back to Cicero, that not everything that passes as law (*lex*) necessarily is so. "Although in the broadest sense of the term everything which may be read is law, nevertheless, in a special sense it signifies a rightful warrant enjoining what is honest, forbidding the contrary."[76] The fact seems to be that Bracton is struggling to adjust the notion of legislative sovereignty, conveyed by the texts of Roman law, to his own desire to subordinate to the law the royal power in its more usual aspects. Blackstone, five hundred years later, is troubled by a like dilemma.

But what sanction does Bracton supply to his law as against

[74] BRACTON, *op. cit. supra* note 72, at ff. 1, 1b.   [75] *Ibid.* f. 107b.
[76] *Ibid.* f. 2; see note 22, *supra.*

the King? In the printed text of the *De Legibus* there is a passage which declares that not only is the King below God, but that he has also his court, namely, counts and barons, and that "he who has an associate has a master, and, therefore, if the King be without a bridle, that is without law, they ought to put a bridle upon him." [77] These words have been sometimes set down, on the ground of conflict with other passages, as an interpolation, but they easily may be a reminiscence, evoked perhaps by De Montfort's rebellion against Henry III, of chapter sixty-one of *Magna Carta*. That the ordinary remedies are not available against royal injustice, Bracton makes clear. No writ will run against the King, the author of all writs.[78] Through his domination of his judges, he may even bring about unjust judgments.[79] And while the King is subject to the law, yet if he orders an official to do wrong, the official can plead the royal order.[80] Also the official shares the royal immunity from jurisdiction and may be complained against only to the King or to those appointed by the King for the purpose.[81] Bracton has, in brief, no idea of the modern concept of the "rule of law." In the last analysis, he intimates, the sole redress against tyranny is reliance on divine vengeance, though doubtless this might operate through human agency.[82] Thus the problem of providing an institutional control upon the acts of the King is left

[77] *Ibid.* f. 34. See Maitland's comment in BRACTON, *op. cit. supra* note 71, at 29–33.

[78] "Sumoneri non potest per breve." *Ibid.* f. 382b. *Cf.* ff. 5b and 171b. See also EHRLICH, PROCEEDINGS AGAINST THE CROWN (6 Oxford Studies in Leg. and Soc. Hist. 1921) 23, 26, 45, 54.

[79] BRACTON, DE LEGIBUS ET CONSUETUDINIBUS ANGLIAE ff. 368b, 369.

[80] EHRLICH, *op. cit. supra* note 78, at 129.

[81] *Ibid.* 111.

[82] DE LEGIBUS ET CONSUETUDINIBUS ANGLIAE f. 369. The origin of the maxim that "the King can do no wrong" has been assigned by some authorities to the minority of Henry III; but if the saying existed in Bracton's day, it meant nearly the opposite of what it does today. "If the king, or anybody else, said that the king 'could not' do something, that meant, not that the act would not, if done, be attributed to the king, but that the king was no more allowed to do it, than a subject was allowed to commit a trespass or a felony." EHRLICH, *op. cit. supra* note 78, at 127.

29

in the *De Legibus* exactly where it is left by the Continental writings of the period. The measure of such control should be the law, and Bracton's conception of this is full and definite; but the institution capable of applying this test with regularity and precision has not yet disclosed itself.

From the *De Legibus* we turn to *Magna Carta* and in so doing from the legal tradition of higher law to the political. Coke was eventually to bring the two together in his presentation of *Magna Carta* as "a restoration and declaration of the ancient common law"; [83] but before this notion could become plausible, *Magna Carta* had to become absorbed into the common law.

The constitutional fathers regarded *Magna Carta* as having been from the first a muniment of English liberties, but the view of it adopted by modern scholarship is a decidedly different one. This is that *Magna Carta* was to begin with a royal grant to a limited class of beneficiaries, and more or less at the expense of the realm at large. The king promised his barons that henceforth he would not infringe their customary feudal privileges as he had done in the immediate past, even though many of these were by no means accordant with the best interests of the remainder of his subjects.[84]

The eventual rôle, indeed, of *Magna Carta* in the history of American constitutional theory is due immediately to its revival at the opening of the seventeenth century, largely by Sir Edward Coke. The tradition which Coke revived was, however, by no means his own invention; it referred back to and was to a great extent substantiated by an earlier period in the history of this famous document—famous especially because it was a *document* and so gave definite, tangible embodiment to the notion of higher law.

From the first, *Magna Carta* evinced elements of growth, and it was fortunately cast into a milieu favoring growth. For one thing, its original form was not that of an enactment, but of a

[83] Co. Inst. I, 8; *ibid.* II, 81; *cf.* 2 Hansard, Parliamentary History (1628) 333.

[84] Adams, Origin of the English Constitution (1912) c. 5; McIlwain, The High Court of Parliament and Its Supremacy (1910) 54 *et seq.*

compact. It is, therefore, significant that when John sought escape from his solemn promises, he turned to the Pope; and while his suit was immediately successful, subsequent confirmation restored the impaired obligation in full force. Far more important is it that certain of the Charter's clauses, like those of the Fourteenth Amendment six hundred and fifty years later, were drawn in terms that did not confine their application to the immediate issues in hand or to the interests therein involved; while to match this feature of the document itself came the early discovery by the baronage that the successful maintenance of the Charter against the monarch demanded the co-operation of all classes and so the participation by all classes in its benefits. Then, toward the close of the thirteenth century, the king, no longer able to "live off his own," eked out by the customary feudal revenues, was forced to call Parliament into existence to relieve his financial necessities. Parliament's subventions, however, were not to be had for the asking, but were conditioned on, among other things, the monarch's pledge to maintain *Magna Carta*.[85] And all this took place, it must be again remembered, in an age whose thought was permeated with the idea of authority limited by law. Had *Magna Carta* been the source of this idea, or the sole expression of it, it must soon have disappeared. Its very different fate testifies to the fact that it not only supported but was also supported by the universal tradition.

For the history of American constitutional law and theory no part of *Magna Carta* can compare in importance with chapter twenty-nine: [86]

[85] ADAMS, *op. cit. supra* note 84, particularly at 160n., 162 *et seq.;* McIlwain, *Magna Carta and Common Law* in MAGNA CARTA COMMEMORATION ESSAYS (Malden ed. 1917) 156–60.

[86] "Nullus liber homo capiatur vel imprisonetur aut disseisiatur de libero tenemento suo vel libertatibus vel liberis consuetudinibus suis aut utlagetur aut exuletur aut aliquo modo destruatur nec super eum ibimus nec super eum mittemus, nisi per legale judicium parium suorum vel per legem terrae." Compare the issue of 1225 and caption 39 of the original issue. It is the later issue which "became the Great Charter of English law." ADAMS, *op. cit. supra* note 84, at 282. It was also called "Magna Charta."

No free man shall be taken or imprisoned or deprived of his freehold or of his liberties or free customs, or outlawed, or exiled, or in any manner destroyed, nor shall we go upon him, nor shall we send upon him, except by a legal judgment of his peers or by the law of the land.

Our present interest in this famous text is confined to its opening phrase, *"nullus liber homo,"* a term evidently intended to indicate the beneficiaries of the clause, perhaps of the Charter as a whole. Although the words *liber homo* may have designated at first few outside the vassal class,[87] in this as in other respects the Charter early manifested its capacity for growth. The second issue of the Charter in 1225 was contemporaneously described as conceding their liberties alike "to people and to populace *(tam populo quam plebi)."* [88] A quarter century later we find the term "common liberties" being used to characterize the subject matter of the Charter.[89] Even more striking is Bracton's term for it—*"constitutio libertatis"* [90]—a phrase which, wittingly or not, attributes to the Charter the consolidation of all particular liberties into *one* liberty. Once again we encounter a form of words of greatest interest to the student of American constitutional law and theory. It is noted at the moment for the evidence it affords of the final and complete emergence of *Magna Carta* from its feudal chrysalis.

Nor did *Magna Carta* develop solely along one dimension. As the range of classes and interests brought under its protection widened, its quality as higher law binding in some sense upon government in all its phases steadily strengthened until it becomes possible to look upon it in the fourteenth century as

---

[87] ADAMS, *op. cit. supra* note 84, at 265; MCILWAIN, *op. cit. supra* note 85, at 80–81, 170.

[88] MCILWAIN, *op. cit. supra* note 85, at 171. In 1354 it was enacted (28 EDW. III, c. 3) that *"no man of what estate or condition he may be* [nul homme, de quel estate ou condicion qil soit], shall be put out of land or tenement, nor taken, nor imprisoned, nor disinherited, nor put to death, without being brought to answer by due process of law." 1 STAT. REALM 345.

[89] MCILWAIN, *op. cit. supra* note 85, at 172.

[90] BRACTON, DE LEGIBUS ET CONSUETUDINIBUS ANGLIAE f. 168b. He also terms it simply "Constitutio," *ibid.* 169b.

something very like a written constitution in the modern understanding. By his *Confirmatio Cartarum* of 1297, Edward I ordered all "justices, sheriffs, mayors, and other ministers, which under us and by us have the laws of our land to guide," to treat the Great Charter as "common law," in all pleas before them. Furthermore, any judgment contrary to the Great Charter or the Charter of the Forest was to be "holden for nought"; and all archbishops and bishops were to pronounce "the sentence of Great Excommunication against all those that by deed, aid, or counsel" proceeded "contrary to the aforesaid charters" or in any point transgressed them.[91] The conception of *Magna Carta* as higher law reached its culmination in the reign of Edward III. Of the thirty-two royal confirmations of the Charter noted by Coke, fifteen occurred in this reign,[92] while near the end of it, in 1368, to the normal form of confirmation the declaration was added by statute that any statute passed contrary to *Magna Carta* "soit tenuz p'nul." [93]

The glorious epoch of *Magna Carta* is the century stretching from the confirmation of Edward I to the deposition of Richard II. Another hundred years and the Charter is found rarely mentioned, while from then on the obscurity in which it is wrapped becomes ever denser, till the anti-Stuart revival of it at the opening of the seventeenth century. For the later and longer portion of this period the explanation is simply Tudor despotism. As the biographer of Henry VIII points out, Shakespeare's *King John* contains not an allusion to *Magna Carta*.[94] For the period antedating the Tudors the explanation is less simple,

[91] ADAMS AND STEPHENS, SELECT DOCUMENTS OF ENGLISH HISTORY (1911) 86–87.

[92] Of these later confirmations Adams writes: "They express not so much a desire that specific provisions of the Charter should be reaffirmed . . . as a desire to get the king's acknowledgment in general that he was bound by the law." ADAMS, *op. cit. supra* note 84, at 289–90n.

[93] 42 EDW. III c. 1 (1368); 1 STAT. REALM 388 (1368); 3 CO. INST. 111; also 1 *ibid.* 81.

[94] POLLARD, HENRY VIII (1905) 35. But, as Pollard notes, allusion was made to the Charter in the proceedings against Wolsey for *Praemunire;* and a translation of *Magna Carta* by one George Ferrers was printed in London in 1541. *Ibid.* 35.

but in general it consists in the fact that almost from its appearance *Magna Carta* was in process of absorption into the general stream of the common law. Bracton regards *Magna Carta* as a statute, part and parcel of the entire body of law of which he is treating. Edward I, as we have seen, ordered his judges to give *Magna Carta,* in causes coming before them, the force and effect of common law. The circumstances of the Wars of the Roses aided the same development. The particular guardian of the integrity and identity of *Magna Carta* was Parliament; but with the extermination of the old nobility, Parliament ceased practically to exist till the Tudors recreated it out of their own adherents. On the other hand, at a time when people did not know from day to day whether Lancaster or York sat on the throne, the common law courts continued for the most part in the discharge of their proper business.[95] It resulted that, as Englishmen recognized in the daily practice of the courts an actual realization of most that *Magna Carta* had symbolized, they transferred to the common law as a whole the worship which they had so long reserved more especially for the Charter.

Writing with this period particularly in mind, Father Figgis has remarked:

The Common Law is pictured invested with a halo of dignity peculiar to the embodiment of the deepest principles and to the highest expression of human reason and of the law of nature implanted by God in the heart of man. As yet men are not clear that an Act of Parliament can do more than declare the Common Law. It is the Common Law which men set up as an object of worship. They regard it as the symbol of ordered life and disciplined activities, which are to replace the license and violence of the evil times now passed away. . . . The Common Law is the perfect ideal of law; for it is natural reason developed and expounded by a collective wisdom of many generations.

95 For some evidence of interruption by sporadic violence, consult the PASTON LETTERS (Fenn ed. 1873) *passim.* Magna Charta is "part of the common law and the ancient law of this kingdom," 2 HANSARD, PARLIAMENTARY HISTORY 333 (1628). "The King cannot dispense with Magna Charta, which is incorporated into the Common Law." 6 COMYN, DIGEST (Dublin ed. 1793) 35 tit. *Praeogative,* D. 7, citing 2 ROL. 115.

. . . Based on long usage and almost supernatural wisdom, its authority is above, rather than below that of Acts of Parliament or royal ordinances which owe their fleeting existence to the caprice of the King or to the pleasure of councillors, which have a merely material sanction and may be repealed at any moment.[96]

The spokesman *par excellence* of this attitude is Sir John Fortescue, Henry VI's Chief Justice, who followed his king into exile and there prepared his famous work. This is his *Praises of the Laws of England*,[97] the importance of which, slight as is the toll of its pages, is abundantly attested by Coke's and Blackstone's repeated citations of it, not to mention the unqualified adoption by both these writers of its estimate of English legal customs and institutions. The *De Laudibus* is, however, no mere ratification of past pieties; it contributes elements of the greatest importance to the development of Anglo-American constitutional theory. Written in France, it stresses the contrast between French autocracy and what Fortescue terms the "mixed political government" of England. The former is treated as sheer usurpation. Inasmuch as the people submitted themselves in the first place to royal authority only in order to preserve their properties and persons, he argues, it is clear that they could never have assented to absolute power

[96] Figgis, Divine Right of Kings (2d ed. 1914) 228–30. "The common law is the absolute perfection of reason." 2 Co. Inst. 179. The common law, "having a principle of growth and progress in itself . . . is already . . . the most complete and admirable system of law—the most healthy and vigorous in its principles, the most favorable to civil liberty, standing the nearest to the divine law, and the best fitted to be the auxiliary and helper of religion itself in the government of individual men and of human society—that has ever existed on earth." Barnard, Discourse on the Life, Character, and Public Services of Ambrose Spencer (1849) 52. See also Adams, *op. cit. supra* note 84, *passim*.

[97] Fortescue, De Laudibus Legum Angliae (Amos ed. 1825). This edition follows Francis Gregor's translation of 1775—sometimes too faithfully. At the close of chapter 34, at 128, Fortescue is made by both editors to say: "It is not a restraint, but rather a liberty to govern a people by the just regularity of a *political* government, or rather right reason." No equivalent of the last four words appears in the Latin original. The page references here are to the 1825 Amos edition.

35

and yet "if not from them, the King could have no such power rightfully at all." [98] Thus, as in Locke two centuries later, the notion of authority as limited is based on the notion of its popular origin. The laws of England, consequently, do not admit of the maxim, *quod principi placuit;* on the contrary, the king can neither "change the laws thereof nor take from the people what is theirs against their consent"; [99] and these laws "in all cases, declare in favor of liberty, the gift of God to man in his creation." [100]

Nor was liberty the only fruit of English institutions, for to this in turn was English prosperity directly traceable. A quaint passage of the *De Laudibus* reads:

Every inhabitant is at his liberty fully to use and enjoy whatever his farm produceth, the fruits of the earth, the increase of his flock, and the like: all the improvements he makes, whether by his own proper industry, or of those he retains in his service, are his own to use and enjoy without the let, interruption, or denial of any: if he be in any wise injured, or oppressed, he shall have his *amends* and satisfaction against the party offending: hence it is, that the inhabitants are rich in gold, silver, and in all the necessaries and conveniences of life. They drink no water, unless at certain times, upon a religious score, and by way of doing penance. They are fed, in great abundance, with all sorts of flesh and fish, of which they have plenty everywhere; they are clothed throughout in good woollens; their bedding and other furniture in their houses are of wool, and that in great store; they are also well provided with all other sorts of household goods and necessary implements for husbandry: every one, according to his rank, hath all things which conduce to make life easy and happy . . . they are treated with mercy and justice, according to the laws of the land; neither are they impleaded in point of property, or arraigned for any capital crime, how heinous soever, but before the king's judges, and according to the laws of the land. These are the advantages consequent from that *political mixed government* which obtains in *England*. . . .[101]

[98] FORTESCUE, DE LAUDIBUS LEGUM ANGLIAE c. 14, at 41. See also *ibid.* 26, 38, 126.

[99] *Ibid.* cc. 9, 13, 18, 34, 36, at 26–27, 38, 55, 125, 136. The expression "Representatives in Parliament" occurs at 55.

[100] *Ibid.* c. 42, at 157.   [101] *Ibid.* c. 36, at 136–38.

And as English legal institutions supported English prosperity, so English prosperity supported them. In no other country in the world, Fortescue contends, would trial by a jury of the vicinage be feasible, for the simple reason that in no other country would there be a sufficient number of honest men of the neighborhood capable of undertaking the service.[102]

But the distinctive contribution of the *De Laudibus* has still to be mentioned, that feature of it which discriminates it sharply from all earlier eulogies of higher law. This is Fortescue's conception of the law as a professional mystery, as the peculiar science of bench and bar. Almost at the outset he asserts the identity of "perfect justice" with "legal justice." [103] Later, through the mouth of his chief interlocutor, the chancellor, he develops the same thought at length.[104] The laws of England, he says, involve two distinct constituents: first, customs, statutes, or acts of Parliament, and the law of nature, all of which correspond to Aristotle's "elements of natural things"; secondly, "maxims," "principles which do not admit of proof by reason and argument," but carry with them their own evidence, and which correspond to that same philosopher's "efficient causes." But the knowledge which men in general have of either of these categories of legal learning is, and can be, but superficial, comparable with that which they have of "faith, love, charity, the sacraments, and God's commandments," while leaving "other mysteries in Divinity to those who preside in the Church." Nor is the case of the ruler himself different from that of the generality of his subjects in this respect; wherefore the chancellor is made to say:

My Prince, there will be no occasion for you to search into the arcana

102 *Ibid.* cc. 25, 26, 29, especially at 91, 104–05. In chapter 27, at 93, occurs the famous sentiment that "one would much rather that twenty guilty persons should escape the punishment of death, than that one innocent person should be condemned, and suffer capitally." Fortescue's complacency with English institutions, as well as his contempt for French, is most amusingly illustrated by his comment on "modern French," that "it is not the same with that used by our lawyers in the *Courts of Law,* but is much altered and depraved by common use." *Ibid.* 78.

103 *Ibid.* c. 4, at 11.   104 *Ibid.* c. 8, at 20.

of our laws with such tedious application and study. . . . It will not be convenient by severe study, or at the expense of the best of your time, to pry into nice points of law: such matters may be left to your judges and counsel . . . ; furthermore, you will better pronounce judgment in the courts by others than in person, it being not customary for the Kings of England to sit in court or pronounce judgment themselves. [*Proprio ore nullus regum Angliae judicium proferre usus est.*]

I know very well the quickness of your apprehension and the forwardness of your parts; but for that expertness in the laws the which is requisite for judges the studies of twenty years [*viginti annorum lucubrationes*] barely suffice.[105]

The colloquy thus imagined by Fortescue was enacted in solemn earnest one hundred and thirty years later. On Sunday morning, November 10, 1608, Coke and "all the judges of England, and the Barons of the Exchequer" faced James I at Hampton Court to confute the notion which had been instilled in him by Archbishop Bancroft that, inasmuch as the judges were but his delegates, he was entitled to decide cases in his own person. "The judges informed the King," Coke records, "that no King after the Conquest assumed to himself to give any judgment in any cause whatsoever, which concerned the administration of justice within this realm, but these were solely determined in the courts of justice. . . ." To this the king answered that "he thought the law was founded on reason, and that he and others had reason, as well as the Judges"; but Coke pointed out the fallacy of this view in the following words:

True it was, that God had endowed his Majesty with excellent science, and great endowments of nature; but his Majesty was not learned in the laws of his realm of England, and causes which concern the life, or inheritance, or goods, or fortunes of his subjects, are not to be

[105] *Ibid.* c. 8. On this subject see an excellent note by Amos in FORTESCUE, *op. cit. supra* note 97, at 23–25; see also 2 CO. INST. 56. Bodin recognized that the Prince ought not to administer justice in person. BLUNTSCHLI, THEORY OF THE STATE (1895) 517. For Bracton's very different view, see DE LEGIBUS ET CONSUETUDINIBUS ANGLIAE f. 107. Edward III endeavored to make royal interference with the course of justice impossible.

decided by natural reason, but by the artificial reason and judgment of the law, which law is an act which requires long study and experience, before that a man can attain to the cognizance of it; and that the law was the golden met-wand and measure to try the causes of the subjects; and which protected his Majesty in safety and peace.

"The King," the report continues, "was greatly offended," saying that "then he should be under the law, which was treason to affirm," to which Coke responded in Bracton's words: *"Quod Rex non debet esse sub homine, sed sub Deo et lege."* [106]

We are thus brought back to a question raised earlier: By what methods was the supremacy of the common law maintained against the royal power? Or to phrase the same question somewhat differently: By what methods was "higher law" kept "positive"? In Bracton's day, as we have seen, there was no regular remedy available to a subject who deemed himself to have been wronged by the king or by the king's officials; but in this respect institutional improvement in the course of the century following was notable. In the first place, as to his lower officials Edward I began the policy of waiving their, that is *his,* immunity. By chapter thirteen òf the statute of Westminster II, enacted in 1285, persons illegally imprisoned by sheriffs were given complete recovery as if the authors of the wrong had no official capacity.[107] Still more important was the development during the same reign of the so-called petition of right.[108] Such

[106] Prohibitions del Roy, 7 Co. 63–65 (1609). "Law was to an important extent conceived by both governors and governed as a subject of science, capable of being learnt by special study, but not capable of being altered by the mere arbitrary will of government, any more than the principles or conclusions of mathematics." SIDGWICK, ELEMENTS OF POLITICS (2d ed. 1897) 652–53, quoted in McILWAIN, HIGH COURT OF PARLIAMENT (1910) 47. "A portion, and a very large portion, of that justice which it belongs to God alone to dispense with exact and unerring equity, is committed to them [judges] to administer." BARNARD, *loc. cit. supra* note 96.

[107] EHRLICH, *op. cit. supra* note 78, at 111.

[108] *Ibid.* 82–96, *passim; ibid.* 179–88. For an ancient fiction dating from the time of Edward I, supporting the courts on the ground of right and usage in the jurisdiction acquired by petition, see *ibid.* 54.

a petition might be addressed to the king, his chancellor, or his council. On the granting of it, the issues raised were determined by the chancellor, the council, the Exchequer, or the King's Bench, and in accordance with the law; [109] since, when the king sued or consented to be sued, he was considered a party and nothing more.[110] The climax of this development was reached in 1346, when Edward III having instructed his justices that they should not, on account of any letters or orders purporting to come from him, "omit to do right," a proviso to that effect was inserted in the oath of the justices.[111] Hence, royal acts and royal claims were brought constantly to the test of the ordinary law, and often as administered by the ordinary courts.

Such a system was certainly not far from realizing the modern conception of the rule of law. There were, nevertheless, facts of a contrary tendency that must not be overlooked. For one thing, the king was recognized by the courts themselves to be in many instances above the law by virtue of his prerogative, and that for the common good.[112] Again, the judges who decided such matters were the king's appointees and held their offices at his pleasure. Yet again, one of these prerogatives was a quite undefined power of rendering statutes ineffective, called the "dispensing power." Lastly, and most important of all, shortly after 1500 theories gained currency which claimed for the king, at least in his legislative capacity, complete independence from every legal restraint. It was the clash of facts and theories such as these with the notion of a higher law which filled English history in the seventeenth century, and it was forces emergent from this clash which projected the notion of higher law across the Atlantic into eighteenth century America.

[III]

It was the happy strategy of the Tudors to convert Parliament from an outpost against the royal power into its active instrument. The result of this alliance for English constitutional ideas was momentous. Contemporaneously Bodin was

109 *Ibid.* 107, 120.   110 *Ibid.* 108.   111 *Ibid.* 131.
112 *Ibid.* 17–19, 40–41, 51, 56–64, 131–41.

attributing to the king of France the whole power of the state and describing that power as "perpetual and absolute," as *"legibus soluta."* [1] Very different is the doctrine of Sir Thomas Smith in his *Commonwealth of England,* written near the middle of Elizabeth's reign:

> The most high and absolute power of the realme of Englande, consisteth in the Parliament. . . . That which is doone by this consent is called firme, stable, and *sanctum,* and is taken for lawe. The Parliament abrogateth olde lawes, maketh newe . . . and hath the power of the whole realme, both the head and the body. For everie Englishman is entended to bee there present, either in person or by procuration and attornies.[2]

In consequence of the Tudor reformation, the joint work of king and Parliament, the concept of sovereignty in the sense of *potestas legibus soluta* became confined to that branch of his power which the king customarily exercised "by and with the advice and consent" of Parliament.

Yet to begin with, this characteristically English compromise was assailed from both sides. The Stuarts, not enjoying the co-operation of Parliament, sought to put themselves beyond the need of it by appealing to the doctrine of the divine right of kings. In answer, their Parliamentary opponents did not hesitate to challenge, in the name of the supremacy of the common law, the outstanding constitutional result of the Tudor reformation; and the foremost figure of this reaction was Sir Edward Coke.

Coke was best known to our ancestors as the commentator on Littleton's *Tenures.* "Coke's Lyttleton," wrote Jefferson many years afterward with reference to the pre-Revolutionary period,

---

[1] 2 Dunning, History of Political Theories (1916) 96 *et seq.*

[2] Smith, De Republica Anglorum (Alston ed. 1906) bk. ii, c. 1. Coke regards the bulk of the law of his time, both common and statute, as unalterable. 2 Co. Inst. 187. "The People of England, have both ancient Fundamental Rights, Liberties, Franchises, Laws, and a Fundamental Government, which like the Laws of the Medes and Persians, neither may nor ought to be altered." Prynne, Good Old Fundamental Liberties (1655) pt. 1, 27.

"was the universal lawbook of students, and a sounder Whig never wrote, nor of profounder learning in the orthodox doctrines of the British Constitution, or in what was called British liberties." [3] Before he was a commentator on the law of England, however, Coke was successively law reporter, crown attorney, chief justice of the Common Pleas, chief justice of the King's Bench, and member of Parliament; and always he was Edward Coke, an outstanding, aggressive personality, with a fixed determination to make himself mightily felt in whatever place of authority he might occupy. That such a person, having occasion to express himself from the standpoint of such various capacities, should be altogether self-consistent, would be demanding too much. Medievalist and legalist, Coke's objective is sharply political—the curbing of the pretensions of royalty. So precedent and authority—the legalist's stock materials— must be bent to the selected end. Indeed, if occasion require, they may be embroidered upon somewhat, for Coke's outlook upon such procedures is not unlike that of a medieval chronicler of edifying intent. In another respect, too, Coke is thoroughly medieval; his method, even in his *Institutes,* is irritatingly fragmentary, with the result that his larger ideas have often to be dug out and pieced together from a heterogeneous mass. Nor should the student of Coke fail to reckon on the difficulty which arises from the sheer operation of time on the significance of the terms which he employs. Madison's warning centuries later against "those errors which have their source in the changed meaning of words and phrases," is singularly pertinent in this instance.[4]

While Coke as attorney general had shown himself conspicuously subservient to the royal interest, his clashes as judge with

[3] 12 JEFFERSON, WRITINGS (Mem. ed. 1903) iv. As a student himself, Jefferson entertained a very uncomplimentary opinion of Coke. 4 *id.* 3.

[4] See especially MacKay, *Coke—Parliamentary Sovereignty or the Supremacy of the Law?* (1924) 22 MICH. L. REV. 215–47; and 5 HOLDSWORTH, HISTORY OF ENGLISH LAW (1924) 423–93. WALLACE, REPORTERS (3d ed. 1855) 112–42, makes a convincing defense of Coke's reliability as a reporter.

James I make a notable chapter in judicial history. His basic doctrine was "that the King hath no prerogative, but that which the law and the land follows," [5] and that of this the judges and not the king were the authorized interpreters.[6] The circumstances of his admonition to James that he had no right to judge as between subject and subject save through the ordinary courts proceeding without royal interference were reviewed above. Later he had cause to inform James that the latter could not by proclamation "make a thing unlawful which was permitted by the law before." [7] On these occasions Coke had the support of his judicial brethren; but in the matter of the Commendams they deserted him to a man. The question put the judges was whether, in a case pending before them which the king thought "to concern him either in power or profit," they could be required to stay proceedings till the king could consult with them. All but Coke answered yes. Coke's answer was "that when that case should be, he would do that which should be fit for a judge to do." [8] Shortly after he was removed from his chief justiceship.

For students of the origins of American constitutional law and theory, however, no judicial utterance of Coke's—few indeed in language—can surpass in interest and importance his

[5] Proclamations, 12 Co. 74, 76 (1611).

[6] Nicholas Fuller's Case, 12 Co. 41 (1608); The Case of the King's Prerogative in Saltpetre, 12 Co. 12 (1607); Case of Non Obstante, or Dispensing Power, 12 Co. 18 (c. 1607). In Commissions of Enquiry, 12 Co. 31 (1608), Coke, commenting on Bates' Case, 2 How. St. Tr. 371 (1606), sustains the King's power to exact retaliatory duties from foreign merchants, and also his power to exact benevolences. Exaction of Benevolence, 12 Co. 119, 120 (c. 1610). See also 2 Co. INST. 63. Today the royal prerogative is subject absolutely to the legislative power of Parliament, and when a statute has directed the exercise of the prerogative in a certain way there is no "remnant prerogative." See Morgan, *Introduction* in ROBINSON, PUBLIC AUTHORITIES AND LEGAL LIABILITY (1925) xiv. See CHITTY, PREROGATIVES OF THE CROWN (1820) 383, for statement of the older view.

[7] Proclamations, 12 Co. 74, 75 (1611).

[8] The Case of Commendams, Hobart 140–66 (1616); HICKS, MEN AND BOOKS (1921) 67–70.

so-called dictum in *Dr. Bonham's Case*, which was decided by the Court of Common Pleas in 1610.[9] Holding that the London College of Physicians was not entitled, under the act of Parliament which it invoked in justification, to punish Bonham for practicing medicine in the city without its license, Coke said:

And it appears in our books, that in many cases, the common law will controul acts of parliament, and sometimes adjudge them to be utterly void: for when an act of parliament is against common right and reason, or repugnant, or impossible to be performed, the common law will controul it and adjudge such act to be void.[10]

In these words we have foreshadowed not merely the power which American courts today exercise in the disallowance of statutes on the ground of their conflict with the Constitution, but also that very test of "reasonableness" which is the ultimate flowering of this power. We must determine if we can to what extent Coke's own intention sanctions the modern application of his doctrine, and also to what extent the historical background of the dictum does so.

We may first dispose of a matter having only incidental reference to these questions. In employing the phrase "common right and reason," Coke is no doubt again alluding to "that artificial reason and judgment of the law" of which he regarded bench and bar as the especial custodians. What is pertinent to note here is that his employment of these terms is by no means the narrowly official and precisionist one that it would probably have been a hundred years before. Early in the sixteenth century the author of *Doctor and Student,* possibly voicing the suspicion of the Tudor epoch toward principles restrictive of

[9] 8 Co. 107a (1610), 2 Brownl. 225 (1610).

[10] 8 Co. 118a (1610). The best comment on the dictum is to be found in McILWAIN, HIGH COURT OF PARLIAMENT AND ITS SUPREMACY (1910) c. 4, and Plucknett, *Bonham's Case and Judicial Review* (1926) 40 HARV. L. REV. 30 *et seq*. COXE, JUDICIAL POWER AND UNCONSTITUTIONAL LEGISLATION (1893) cc. 13–17 is of incidental value. Ellesmere's charge that Coke had the support of only one judge and that three others were against him seems to be refuted both by Coke's and by Brownlow's report of the case. Apparently only three judges participated, and all agreed with Coke's statement.

governmental authority, had taken pains to explain that the term "law of nature" "is not used among them that be learned in the laws of England." [11] The attitude revealed by Coke and his associates contemporaneously with *Bonham's Case* is very different. Reporting *Calvin's Case,* which was decided the same year, following argument by the chief legal lights of England, Coke says, by way of summary: "1. That ligeance or obedience of the subject to the Sovereign is due by the law of nature: 2. That this law of nature is part of the laws of England: 3. That the law of nature was before any judicial or municipal law in the world: 4. That the law of nature is immutable, and cannot be changed." [12] He then recites in support of these propositions the following quaint argument:

The law of nature is that which God at the time of creation of the nature of man infused into his heart, for his preservation and di-

[11] St. Germain, Doctor and Student (Muchall ed. 1787) 12–13. Suspicion of ecclesiastical domination is given by Pollock as the reason for the reluctance of the sages of the common law before the Reformation to refer expressly to the laws of nature. Pollock, Expansion of the Common Law (1904) 112–13. Fortescue, however, evinced no such reluctance. Bryce notes that both Yelverton and Lord Chancellor Stillington, who held office under Edward IV, referred to the law of nature. Bryce, Studies in History and Jurisprudence (1901) 601. Pollock himself adds: "It is not credible that a doctrine which pervaded all political speculation in Europe, and was assumed as a common ground of authority by the opposing champions of the Empire and the Papacy, should have been without influence among learned men in England." Bryce, *loc. cit. supra.* See also Pollock, *History of the Law of Nature* in his Essays in the Law (1922) 157; Lowell, Government of England (1908) 480–88. 4 Holdsworth, History of English Law 276, 279–82; 5 *ibid.* 216, points out the close connection between equity and the law of nature in the fifteenth and sixteenth centuries. Though equity never served the purposes of a higher law, restrictive of royal or Parliamentary authority, it may have helped to keep natural law ideas alive for that use in the seventeenth century. The adaptability of the common law was referred in the nineteenth century to its resting upon the law of nature. See argument of Alexander Hamilton in People v. Croswell, 3 Johns. 337 (N. Y. 1804); also Barnard, Discourse on the Life, Character, and Public Services of Ambrose Spencer (1849) 52. Thus the applied law changes through the progressive revelation to the judges of the immutable law.

[12] 7 Co. 1, 4b (1610).

rection; and this is *Lex aeterna,* the moral law, called also the law of nature. And by this law, written with the finger of God in the heart of man, were the people of God a long time governed before the law was written by Moses, who was the first reporter or writer of law in the world. . . . And Aristotle, nature's Secretary Lib. 5. Æthic. saith that *jus naturale est, quod apud omnes homines eandem habet potentiam.* And herewith doth agree Bracton lib. 1. cap. 5. and Fortescue cap. 8. 12. 13. and 16. *Doctor and Student,* cap. 2. and 4.[13]

The receptive and candid attitude thus evinced toward natural law ideas, a fresh influx of which from the Continent was already setting in, is a matter of profound importance. In the great constitutional struggle with the Stuarts it enabled Coke to build upon Fortescue, and it enabled Locke to build upon Coke. It made allies of sixteenth century legalism and seventeenth century rationalism, and the alliance then struck has always remained, now more, now less vital, in American constitutional law and theory.

The question of the significance which Coke attached to "common rights and reason" can, however, be answered in much more definite terms. Let the reader's mind revert in this connection to those "maxims" which, according to Fortescue, "do not admit of proof by reason and argument" but bear with them their own evidence, and which, according to the same authority, constituted the very substance of the peculiar science of the judges.[14] Coke yields very little to his predecessor in the reverence he pays to such "fundamental points of the common law." [15] It was, moreover, just such a maxim that Coke found to be involved in *Bonham's Case.* The College of Physicians had, under color of authority from an act of Parliament, amerced Bonham and taken half the fine for themselves. Coke's

[13] 7 Co. at 12a–12b. Bacon's argument in the case invoked the law of nature. 2 BACON, WORKS (Montague ed. 1825) 166, 176.

[14] See page 37, *supra. Cf.* ST. GERMAIN, DOCTOR AND STUDENT 25–26.

[15] "In truth they are the main pillars and supporters of the fabric of the Commonwealth." 1 Co. INST. 74. He also issues a warning that "the alteration of any of these maxims of the common law is most dangerous." *Ibid.* 210; see also *ibid.* 97.

comment is as follows: "The censors cannot be judges, ministers, and parties; judges to give sentence or judgment; ministers to make summons; and parties to have the moiety of the forfeiture, quia aliquis non debet esse judex in propria causa; imo iniquum est aliquem suae rei esse judicem." [16] Thereupon follows the famous dictum.

"Common right and reason" is, in short, something fundamental, something permanent; it is higher law. And again it is relevant to note the ratification which Coke's doctrine received in American constitutional law and theory. With such axioms, traceable in many instances to the *Digest* and *Code* of Justinian, Coke's pages abound; [17] and from his work many of them early found their way into American judicial decisions, sometimes as interpretative of the written constitution, sometimes as supplementary of it. Such a postulate is the doctrine that "a statute should have prospective, not retrospective operation." [18] Another is the principle that "no one should be twice punished for the same offence." [19] Another is the maxim that "every man's house is his own castle." [20] Still another is the aphorism which has played so large a rôle in the history of the

[16] "Ne quis in sua causa judicet vel jus sibi dicat." (No man may be a judge in his own cause.) CODE III, 5, 1; WOOLF, BARTOLUS (1913) 159. *Cf.* BRACTON, DE LEGIBUS ET CONSUETUDINIBUS ANGLIAE (Twiss ed. 1854) f. 119; Earl of Derby's Case, 12 Co. 114 (1614); Tumey v. Ohio, 273 U. S. 510 (1926); also cases cited in notes 35 and 37, *infra.*

[17] I have used BROOM, LEGAL MAXIMS (5th Am. ed. 1870). There are earlier collections by Wingate and by Noy.

[18] BROOM, LEGAL MAXIMS 34–35. "Nova constitutio futuris formam imponere debet, non praeteritis." *Cf.* "Leges et constitutiones futuris certum est dare formam negotiis, non ad facta praeterita revocari; nisi nominatim etiam de praeterito tempore adhuc pendentibus negotiis cautum sit." CODE I, 14, 7. In this, the original form, no suggestion of a restriction on the legislative power appears.

[19] "Nemo debet bis puniri pro uno delicto. . . . Deus non agit bis in idipsum." Bonham's Case, 8 Co. 114 (1610). See also Wetherel v. Darly, 4 Co. 40 (1583); Hudson v. Lee, 4 Co. 43 (1589); and BROOM, LEGAL MAXIMS 347.

[20] Semayne's Case, 5 Co. 91 (1605); BROOM, LEGAL MAXIMS 321: "Domus sua cuique est tutissimum refugium." *Cf.* "Nemo de domo sua extrahi debet." DIG. I, 17, 103.

judicial concept of the police power, *"Sic utere tuo ut alienum non laedas"*; [21] while another, almost equally famous in the history of constitutional litigation, is the axiom *"delegata potestas non potest delegari."* [22] Every one of these axioms is citable to the *Reports* or the *Institutes,* and each one was first taken thence, if not from intermediate derivative works, by early American lawyers and judges. Mention might also be made of the numerous rules for the construction of written instruments which were originally adapted from the same sources to the business of constitutional construction.[23]

We are thus brought to the question of Coke's meaning when he speaks of "controuling" an act of Parliament and "adjudging such act to be void." When the Supreme Court of the United States pronounces an act of Congress "void," it ordinarily means void *ab initio,* because beyond the power of Congress to enact, and it furthermore generally implies that it would similarly dispose of any future act of the same tenor. Was Coke laying claim to any such sweeping power for the ordinary courts as against acts of Parliament?

One thing seems to be assured at the outset—Coke was not asserting simply a rule of statutory construction which owed its force to the assumed intention of Parliament as it would today, although the statute involved in *Bonham's Case* was also construed from that point of view.[24] As we have already seen, Coke was enforcing a rule of higher law deemed by him to be binding on Parliament and the ordinary courts alike. This also appears from his treatment of the precedents he adduces. The

[21] Aldred's Case, 9 Co. 57, 59 (1611); BROOM, LEGAL MAXIMS 274. In these places the maxim is considered purely as a rule of private conduct.

[22] 2 CO. INST. 597; BROOM, LEGAL MAXIMS 665, where it is stated as a principle of the law of agency.

[23] See, *e.g.,* BROOM, LEGAL MAXIMS 650, 682.

[24] "An act of parliament . . . (as a will) is to be expounded according to the intention of the makers." 8 Co. 114, 119 (1610). This is said with reference to a comparison of certain clauses of the act before the court. *Cf.* 1 BL. COMM. 91: "Where some collateral matter arises out of the general words, and happens to be unreasonable, there the judges are, in decency, to conclude that this consequence was not foreseen by the Parliament."

most ancient of these is *Tregor's Case,* which occurred in the eighth year of Edward III's reign.[25] On that occasion Chief Justice Herle had used these words: "There are some statutes made which he himself who made them does not will to put into effect"; although just why this is so is not stated. In Coke's opinion these words become: "Some statutes are made against common law and right, which they that made them perceiving would not put into execution." In other words, the law-making body itself recognized the binding and invalidating force of principles external to the legislative act. Two other precedents Coke submits to similar elaboration.[26]

Furthermore, we should recall in this connection, Coke's repeated assertion that statutes made against Magna Carta were "void," a doctrine that Parliament itself had confirmed more than once in annulling its own past enactments.[27] Nor may we overlook his words in the *Case of Non Obstante or the Dispensing Power:* "No act can bind the King from any prerogative which is sole and inseparable to his person, but that he may dispense with it by a *Non obstante;* as a sovereign power to command any of his subjects to serve him for the public weal"; or the sovereign power of pardon, and he instances acts of Parliament itself which recognize this principle.[28] In *Calvin's Case,* decided the term before *Bonham's Case,* the same doctrine is repeated, with the exception that the royal prerogative is rested

[25] McIlwain, High Court of Parliament 286 *et seq.*

[26] Plucknett, *supra* note 10. See also *supra* note 11.

[27] 1 Co. Inst. 81; 2 *id.* 51; 3 *id.* 111; Proclamations, 12 Co. 74, 76 (1611); Ehrlich, Proceedings Against the Crown (6 Oxford Studies in Leg. and Soc. Hist. 1921) 114. In 1341 the Chancellor and others protested that "they could not keep them [certain statutes] in case those statutes were contrary to the laws and customs of the realm, which they were sworn to keep." *Ibid.* 115. In other words, a statute merely as such is not necessarily law of the realm. *Cf.* Proclamations, 12 Co. 74, 76 (1611). The first recorded judicial application of the word "void" in relation to a statute seems to have been in the Annuity Case, in Fitzherbert, Abridgment (Pasch. 27 Hen. VI (1450)), one of the precedents cited by Coke in support of the dictum. Its precise significance, however, in that connection seems to have been uncertain to Coke himself. Coxe, *op. cit. supra* note 10, at 153–60.

[28] 12 Co. 18 (c. 1607).

on the "law of nature." [29] Nor does such doctrine lose in impressiveness when we reflect that along with it, in Coke's mind, went the doctrine that the royal prerogative was subject to delimitation by the common law as applied by the ordinary courts.

At the very least, therefore, we can assert that in *Bonham's Case* Coke deemed himself to be enforcing a rule of construction of statutes of higher intrinsic validity than any act of Parliament as such. Does this, on the other hand, necessarily signify that he regarded the ordinary courts as the *final* authoritative interpreters of such rule of construction? A contemporaneous critic of the dictum in *Bonham's Case* was Lord Chancellor Ellesmere, whose objection was couched in the following significant terms:

He challenged not power for the Judges of this Court [King's Bench] to correct all misdemeanors as well extrajudicial as judicial, nor to have power to judge Statutes and acts of Parliament to be void, if they conceived them to be against common right and reason; but left to the King and Parliament to judge what was common right and reason. I speak not of impossibilities or direct repugnances.[30]

The issue contemporaneously raised by the dictum, therefore, was not, as we should say today, between judicial power and legislative power; but between the law declaring power of the ordinary courts and the like power of "the High Court of Parliament."

There may have been a period when Coke, in view of the threatened deadlock between the king and the Houses, dreamed of giving the law to both through the mouths of the judges. Otherwise it is difficult to account for such criticisms as that voiced by Ellesmere, the accumulation of which was a material factor in forcing Coke's retirement from the Bench six years later. And further confirming this suspicion is, on the one hand, the obviously gratuitous character of the dictum, the case having been adequately disposed of on other grounds, and, on the other hand, Coke's apparent effort later to effect a retreat

[29] 7 Co. 1a, 14a (1609).
[30] McILWAIN, *op. cit. supra* note 10, at 293–94, citing Moore 828 (1663).

from an untenable position. In *Rowles v. Mason,* decided in 1612, Coke stated that the common law "Corrects, Allows, and Disallows, both *Statute Law, and Custom,* for if there be repugnancy in *Statute;* or unreasonablenesse in custom, the Common Law Disallowes and rejects it, as appears by Doctor *Bonhams Case. . . .*" [31] This statement of the matter seems to bring his own theory into line with Ellesmere's. His later expressions in the *Institutes* are in the same tone. Indeed, at one point he asserts, on the authority of Chief Justice Herle, a judge in the reign of Edward III, that an award by the High Court of Parliament is "the highest law that could be." [32]

In brief, while Coke regarded the ordinary courts as peculiarly qualified to interpret and apply the law of reason, he also, finally at least, recognized the superior claims of the High Court of Parliament as a *law declaring body.* Indeed, as we shall see in a moment, his last years were especially devoted to asserting the competence of Parliament in this respect. While the dictum uncovers one of the indispensable premises of the doctrine of judicial review, the other, that which rests on the principle of separation of powers, he still lacks. This, of course, is a matter to be treated later.

A word should be added regarding the reception and transmission of the dictum. Though there is no reference in *Day v. Savadge* [33] to *Bonham's Case,* Chief Justice Hobart's words in the later case are doubtless an echo: "Even an Act of Parlia-

[31] 2 Brownl. 192, 198 (1612). He adds that "statute law . . . corrects, abridges, and explains the Common Law." Notice also his expression in his "Humble and Direct Answer" in explanation of a precedent used in Bonham's Case: "and, because that this is against common right and reason, the common law adjudges the said act of parliament *as to this point* void" (italics mine). 2 BACON, WORKS 506.

[32] 2 CO. INST. 497–98. A still more decisive passage may be found in 4 *id.* 37; *cf.* 1 BL. COMM. 91. See also Co. INST. 272(a) (b); *ibid.* 360(a), 381(b); 2 *id.* 148, 301; *cf.* 6 BACON, ABRIDGMENT (6th ed. 1807) 383, 635, 643. I do not find, however, that Coke anywhere in the INSTITUTES says that a statute may be void in relation to "common right and reason," though he does say that statutes contrary to *Magna Carta* are, and that "words of an act of Parliament must be taken in lawful and rightful sense." 1 CO. INST. 381(b). See also COXE, *op. cit. supra* note 10, at 154–55.

[33] Hobart 85 (1614).

ment, made against Natural Equity, as to make a Man Judge in his own Cause, is void in itself; for *jura naturae sunt immutabĭlia* and they are *leges legum.*" [34] Thus Bracton—and ultimately Cicero—is brought to Coke's support. In *Captain Streater's Case,*[35] decided in 1653, while the Barebones Parliament was in control, the dictum for the first time encountered the rising principle of legislative sovereignty. Streater, who had been arrested on an order by the Parliament, applied for a writ of *habeas corpus* on the ground that such an order was not "law of the land" and so was void. He pleaded that, "Parliaments ever made laws, but judges of the law judged by those laws." The court answered: "Mr. Streater, one must be above another, and the inferior must submit to the superior. . . . If the Parliament should do one thing, and we do the contrary here, things would run round. We must submit to the legislative power. . . ." [36]

Yet even as late as 1701, we find Chief Justice Holt reaffirming the dictum, in the case of *City of London v. Wood,*[37] but not without significant ambiguity. At one point in his opinion, Holt says that the difference between a municipal by-law and an act of Parliament is "that a by-law is liable to have its validity brought in question, but an act of Parliament is not." Yet he later adds:

And what my Lord Coke says in *Dr. Bonham's Case* in his 8 Coke is far from any extravagancy, for it is a very reasonable and true say-

---

[34] *Ibid.* at 87a–87b.   [35] 5 How. St. Tr. 365 (1653).

[36] *Ibid.* at 386. Meantime Finch, C. J., in his LAW (1636), had surpassed the dictum in dogmatic assertion of the legal limits on Parliament's powers. "Therefore Lawes positive, which are directly contrary to the former [the law of reason] lose their force, and are no Lawes at all. As those which are contrary to the law of Nature." FINCH, LAW (1636) bk. 1, c. 6, quoted by Pound, *Common Law and Legislation* (1908) 21 HARV. L. REV. 391–92. In the Ship-Money case, Finch, C. J., advanced a similar doctrine in defence of the royal prerogative. "No act of parliament can bar a king of his regality. . . . Therefore acts of parliament to take away his royal power in defence of the kingdom are void." See MAITLAND, CONSTITUTIONAL HISTORY (1909) 299.

[37] 12 Mod. 678 (1701).

52

ing, That if an act of Parliament should ordain that the same person should be party and judge, or, which is the same thing, judge in his own cause, it would be a void act of Parliament; for it is impossible that one should be judge and party, for the judge is to determine between party and party. . . .[38]

What precisely does Holt mean by the word "impossible" here? Does he mean impossible without injustice; or does he mean impossible without logical absurdity—what Coke himself had termed "repugnancy"—and giving rise perhaps to something approaching physical impossibility? In the one case the restraint on the act of Parliament is still the higher law, in the other it is not. The question cannot be resolved further than to say that Holt, like Blackstone later, seems to be attempting to bridge the gap between two conflicting theories of law. As we shall see, these attempts furnished a useful prop to judicial review in its earlier American stages.[39]

From Holt's time, the dictum finds no place in important judicial opinion in England; but it does find its way into the *Digests* and *Abridgments* of the time, works which are apt to be comprehensive rather than critical. Through these works, as well as the *Reports,* it passed to America to join there the arsenal of weapons being accumulated against Parliament's claims to sovereignty.

In 1616 Coke, who had three years earlier been transferred from the Common Pleas to the King's Bench, was dismissed as judge altogether. Four years later he was elected to the House of Commons, and there at once assumed the leadership of the growing opposition to the Stuarts. In 1625 Charles succeeded James, and in 1627 occurred the arbitrary arrest by royal order of the Five Knights, giving rise in Parliament to the great Inquest on the Liberties of the Subject, and eventually to the framing of the Petition of Right.[40] In all these proceedings the leading rôle fell to Coke, and their general tendency is made clear in the quaint words of Sir Benjamin Rudyard, who ex-

[38] *Ibid.* at 687.   [39] COXE, *op. cit. supra* note 10, at 176–78, and c. 25.
[40] 2 HANSARD, PARLIAMENTARY HISTORY (1628) 262–366.

pressed his great gratification to see "that good, old, decrepit law of Magna Charta, which hath been so long kept in and lain bed-rid, as it were . . . walk abroad again." [41] Coke's main objective was still the curbing of the royal prerogative, but the terms in which he expressed himself also assert the existence of constitutional limits to Parliament's power as well. Especially significant are his remarks on the clause "saving the sovereign power" of the king which was at first attached to the Petition by the Lords. The question arising, "what is Sovereign power," a member quoted Bodin to the effect "that it is free from any conditions"; whereupon Coke arose and said:

This is *magnum in parvo*. . . . I know that prerogative is a part of the law, but "Sovereign Power" is no parliamentary word. In my opinion it weakens Magna Charta, and all the statutes; for they are absolute without any saving of "Sovereign Power"; and should we now add it, we shall weaken the foundation law, and then the building must needs fall. Take heed what we yield unto: Magna Charta is such a fellow, that he will have no "Sovereign." [42]

The words of Wentworth and Pym during the same debate were to like effect. The former said, "These laws are not acquainted with 'Sovereign Power' "; while Pym added that, far from being able to accord the king sovereign power, Parliament itself was "never possessed of it." [43] Another noteworthy feature of the debate was the appearance in the course of it of the word "unconstitutional" in essentially its modern sense when used in political discussion.[44]

In his *Institutes*, Coke, still the embattled commoner, completes his restoration of *Magna Carta* as the great muniment of English liberties. It is called "Magna Charta, not for the length or largeness of it . . . but . . . in respect of the great weighti-

[41] *Ibid.* 335. [42] *Ibid.* 356–57. [43] *Ibid.*

[44] The occasion was Serjeant Ashley's expression of "divine right" sentiment. *Ibid.* 317. "The doctrine advanced by this gentleman seemed so unconstitutional that he was ordered into custody." *Ibid.* 328–29. Chalmers in his POLITICAL ANNALS notes that the word "unconstitutional" was applied in New England to certain acts of Parliament in 1691. 1 NEW YORK HISTORICAL SOCIETY COLLECTIONS (1868) 81.

ness and weighty greatness of the matter contained in it; in a few words, being the fountain of all the fundamental laws of the realm." [45] Declaratory of the common law, "this Statute of Magna Charta hath been confirmed above thirty times." [46] Judgments and statutes against it "shall be void." [47] Its benefits extend to all, even villeins, they being freemen as to all save their own lords.[48] And what are these benefits? Especially they are the benefits of the historical procedure of the common law, the known processes of the ordinary courts, indictment by grand jury, trial by "law of the land," *habeas corpus,* security against monopoly, taxation by the consent of Parliament.[49] Thus the vague concept of "common right and reason" is replaced with a "law fundamental" of definite content and traceable back to one particular document of ancient and glorious origin.

And alongside *Magna Carta* in the pages of the *Institutes* stands "the High Court of Parliament," Coke's description of whose powers has been often interpreted as flatly contradicting his teachings regarding a "law fundamental." "Of the power and jurisdiction of Parliament," runs a famous passage, "for the making of laws in proceeding by bill, it is so transcendent and absolute, as it cannot be confined either for causes or persons within any bounds." [50] A century and a quarter later this same passage was to be quoted by Blackstone as expressing the notion of Parliamentary sovereignty.[51] Actually in Coke's pages it has no such significance. As his own words indicate, he classifies Parliament as primarily a *court,* albeit a court which may make new law as well as declare the old; and what he is describing is not a power and jurisdiction which is entitled to override rights at will, though it is entitled to reach all "persons

---

[45] 1 Co. Inst. 81; 2 Hansard, Parliamentary History 327. See also 2 Co. Inst. 57.

[46] 1 *id.* 36, 81.

[47] See note 27, *supra;* also 4 Bacon, Abridgment (6th ed. 1807) 638.

[48] 2 Co. Inst. 45.

[49] *Ibid.* 2–77, furnishing a general commentary on the charter.

[50] 4 *id.* 36.   [51] 1 Bl. Comm. 160–61.

and causes." [52] Furthermore, the illustrations which he gives of Parliament's "transcendent power and jurisdiction" are not, by today's standards, instances of law-making at all, but of the exercise of a species of equity jurisdiction in individual cases which, while it may seem often to invade the rights of those most immediately affected, was apparently controlled by the motive of vindicating rights of others.

Daughters and heirs apparent . . . may by act of Parliament inherit during the life of the ancestor. It may adjudge an infant or minor of full age. To attaint a man of treason after death. [To attaint a man during life was too ordinary a manifestation of Parliamentary authority to deserve, in Coke's estimate, special mention.] To naturalize a mere alien, and make him a subject born. It may bastard a child that by law is legitimate, the father being a proved adulterer. To legitimize one that is illegitimate. . . .[53]

Clearly, what we have here exemplified is not legislative sovereignty, but rather entire absence of the modern distinction between legislation and adjudication.

That Coke generally regards the cause of Parliament and that of the law as identical is altogether evident. *Magna Carta* itself was of Parliamentary origin, and Parliament had later forced more or less reluctant monarchs to confirm the charter no less than thirty-two times. "A Parliament," he writes, "brings judges, officers and all men into good order. . . . [Note the inclusion of judges in this list.] Parliament and the Common Law are the principal means to keep greatness in order and due subjection." [54]

Coke's contributions to the beginnings of American constitu-

---

[52] McILWAIN, HIGH COURT OF PARLIAMENT 141 *et seq.;* also *ibid.* 312n.; 2 Co. INST. 497–98; 2 HANSARD, PARLIAMENTARY HISTORY 271–312; PEASE, THE LEVELLER MOVEMENT (1916) 43–45. "These two judgments in parliament by way of declaration of law, against which no man can speak." See the *Argument in Calvin's Case* in 2 BACON, WORKS 179.

[53] 4 Co. INST. 36.

[54] 2 *id.* 626; 2 HANSARD, PARLIAMENTARY HISTORY 246. For quaint comparisons of Parliament with a clock and with an elephant, see 4 Co. INST. 2–3.

tional law may be briefly summarized. First, in his dictum in *Bonham's Case* he furnished a form of words which, treated apart from his other ideas, as it was destined to be by a series of judges, commentators, and attorneys, became the most important single source of the notion of judicial review. This is true even though we of the present day can see that, in view of the universal subordination of the common law as such to statute law, judicial review grounded simply on "common right and reason" could not have survived. But, as if in anticipation of this difficulty, Coke came forward with his second contribution, the doctrine of a law fundamental, binding Parliament and king alike, a law, moreover, embodied to great extent in a particular document and having a verifiable content in the customary procedure of everyday institutions. From his version of *Magna Carta,* through the English Declaration and Bill of Rights of 1688 and 1689, to the Bills of Rights of our early American constitutions the line of descent is direct; and if American constitutional law during the last half century has tended increasingly to minimize the importance of procedural niceties and to return to the vaguer tests of "common right and reason," the intervening stage of strict law was nevertheless necessary. Lastly, Coke contributed the notion of Parliamentary supremacy *under* the law, which in time, with the differentiation of legislation and adjudication, became transmutable into the notion of *legislative* supremacy within a law subject to construction by the processes of adjudication.

[IV]

It has become a commonplace that every age has its own peculiar categories of thought; its speculations are carried on in a vocabulary which those who would be understood by it must adopt, and then adapt to their own special purposes. Nowadays intellectual discourse is apt to be cast in the mould of the evolutionary hypothesis. In the seventeenth and eighteenth centuries, the doctrine of natural law, with its diverse corollaries, furnished the basic postulates of theoretical speculation. For this there were several reasons; but our interest is naturally centered upon those which were especially operative in England.

The immense prestige of the natural law doctrine in the seventeenth and eighteenth centuries was due particularly to the work of two men, Grotius and Newton. In erecting the law of nations upon a natural law basis as a barrier against the current international anarchy, Grotius imparted to the latter a new solidity, as well as an immediate practicality such as it had never before been able to boast. Yet even more important was Grotius' revival of the Ciceronian idea of natural law, which served at one stroke to clear the concept from the theological implications which it had accumulated during the Middle Ages and from any suspicion of dependence on ecclesiastical and Papal interpretation. Once again natural law is defined as right reason; and is described as at once a law of, and a law to, God. God himself, Grotius asserted, could not make twice two other than four; nor would his rational nature fail to guide man even though there were no God, or though God lacked interest in human affairs.[55] And at this point Newton enters the story.[56] While modern science employs the term "natural law" in a sense that is alien and even hostile to its juristic use, the vast preponderance of deduction over observation in Newton's discoveries at first concealed this opposition. His demonstration that the force which brings the apple to the ground is the same force that holds the planets in their orbits, stirred his contemporaries with the picture of a universe which is pervaded with the same reason which shines in man and is accessible in all its

[55] 1 GROTIUS, DE JURE BELLI AC PACIS 1, 5, 10; GROTIUS, PROLEGOMENA (Whewell ed. 1853) 11. Von Gierke finds a German precursor of Grotius in Gabriel Biel, who wrote in 1495: "Nam si per impossibile Deus non esset, qui est ratio divina, aut ratio illa divina esset errans: adhuc si quis ageret contra rectam rationem angelicam vel humanam aut aliam aliquam si qua esset: peccaret." GIERKE, ALTHUSIUS (Zur. deutschen Staats u. Rechts Geschichte 1879–80) 74, n.45. Related to this question is the medieval controversy whether *jus naturale* is divine will (*voluntas*) or divine reason (*ratio*), whether God is a law-giver or a teacher working through the reason. GROTIUS, PROLEGOMENA, 73, n.44.

[56] See BECKER, THE DECLARATION OF INDEPENDENCE (1922) 40–53.

parts to exploration by man. Between a universe "lapt in law" and the human mind all barriers were cast down. Inscrutable deity became scrutable nature. On this basis arose English deism, which, it has been wittily remarked, "deified Nature and denatured God." [57] And one section of nature is human nature and its institutions. With Newton's achievement at their back men turned confidently to the formulation of the inherently just and reasonable rules of social and political relationship. Entire systems were elaborated which purported to deduce with Euclidean precision the whole duty of man, both moral and legal, from a few agreed premises.[58] It was the discredit into which such systems ultimately fell that revealed the disparity between the two uses of the term "natural law" of which we today are aware—or should be.[59]

[57] *Ibid.* 51. "The eighteenth century, conceiving of God as known only through his work, conceived of his work as itself a universal harmony, of which the material and the spiritual were but different aspects." *Ibid.* 52–53. Addison's famous Hymn is a fine expression of the deistic cosmology. It is Pope, however, who condensed the deistic philosophy of history into a line: "Whatever is, is right." ESSAY ON MAN (1732) Ep. i, l. 294. The theological classic of Deism is Butler's ANALOGY, where Christianity is presented as "a promulgation of the law of nature . . . with new light . . . adapted to the wants of mankind." 1 BUTLER, WORKS (Gladstone, ed. 1897) 162. Note also Butler's contention that "miracles must not be compared to common natural events . . . but to the extraordinary phenomena of nature." *Ibid.* 181. The later and most extreme representatives of Deism, for example Voltaire and Jefferson, scouted miracles altogether, which led to their being termed "atheists" and "infidels."

[58] See an interesting note in DICKINSON, ADMINISTRATIVE JUSTICE AND SUPREMACY OF LAW (1927) 115–18. See also the same writer's reference to Domat, DICKINSON, *op. cit. supra* 125n. Pufendorf took issue with Grotius' contention that "there is not equal certainty to be met with in morals and mathematics." 1 PUFENDORF, LAW OF NATURE AND NATIONS (Spavan ed. 1716) 2, 9. "Principles of civil knowledge, fairly deduced from the law of nature." WISE, VINDICATION OF THE GOVERNMENT OF NEW ENGLAND CHURCHES (1860) 45.

[59] "Natural Law" in the sense of "the observed order of phenomena" has tended in recent years to crowd the earlier rationalistic conception to the wall, thus aiding the triumph of the idea of human and governmental law as an expression solely of will backed by force. The nineteenth century was no stranger to the idea that there are factors of human behavior

The revived Ciceronian conception of natural law, extended and deepened by Newtonian science, furnishes, therefore, the general background of credibility against which the contemporary political applications of natural law have to be projected. But these political applications also bring into requisition certain new elements—new, that is to say, in the combinations in which they now appear. For it is always a question when theoretical notions are under consideration whether the term "new" is in strict propriety admissible. Systems fall apart and new systems are assembled from the wreckage. Any serious turn of events is apt to produce a fresh coruscation of ideas, elevating some and suppressing others; but the contents of the kaleidoscope remain throughout much the same. And never was this observation better borne out than by the political speculations of the sixteenth, seventeenth, and eighteenth centuries. These speculations contributed immensely to the shattering of the existing foundations of authority and in transferring authority to an entirely new basis. The particular ideas in which they dealt were, nevertheless, for the most part, far from novel. Not a few of them are identifiable, in embryo at least, among the writings of the ancients; and nearly all of them had been stated with varying degrees of clarity before the Reformation.

---

which are obdurate to advantageous political control; only such factors are ordinarily represented as of a non-rational nature and *as having no necessary tendency to produce human justice*. Savigny's apotheosis of custom was an appeal to a natural law of this sub-rational or scientific type. So also were the confident pronouncements of the classical economists regarding the "laws of Political Economy." So again were the characteristic preachments of Herbert Spencer concerning the proper field of governmental intervention, wherein is linked up, with an altogether shameless illogic, the notion of an automatic industrial organism to a revived theory of natural rights. Professor Duguit would also have us regard his "social solidarity" as a scientific datum. In fact, all these theories are only endeavors to dragoon science into the service of some variety or other of Utopism. Professor Duguit's theory, for example, is only that of Locke stood on its head—nor is this to question but that twentieth century conditions may demand this novel perspective.

The conveyance of natural law ideas into American constitutional theory was the work pre-eminently—though by no means exclusively—of John Locke's *Second Treatise on Civil Government,* which appeared in 1690 as an apology for the Glorious Revolution. The outstanding feature of Locke's treatment of natural law is the almost complete dissolution which this concept undergoes through his handling into the natural rights of the individual; or—to employ Locke's own phrase, borrowed from the debates between Stuart adherents and Parliamentarians—into the rights of "life, liberty, and estate." [60] The dissolving agency by which Locke brings this transformation about is the doctrine of the Social Compact, with its corollary notion of a State of Nature. Indeed, it is hardly an exaggeration to say that the only residuum which remains in the Lockian crucible from the original Ciceronian concept is the sanction which is claimed from natural law for the social compact, and at one point, he dispenses even with this. It thus becomes of interest to inquire whence Locke derived his intense preoccupation with rights, as well as the form in which he chose to express them.

A recent effort has been made to refer Locke's system to Calvinistic premises; [61] but if it is meant that the outstanding features of Locke's political thinking are traceable to Calvin himself, the thesis falls of its own weight. Calvin know nothing of the social compact—he rests civil authority on the basis of divine right. Far from being an apologist for revolution, he in general teaches non-resistance. The doctrine of the sovereignty of God which looms so large in his pages bears not the faintest

[60] 2 DUNNING, HISTORY OF POLITICAL THEORIES (1923) 222, 346n. "Is it not a common principle that the law favoureth three things, life, liberty, and dower. . . . This because our law is grounded upon the law of nature. And these three things do flow from the **law** of nature. . . ." Bacon, *Argument in Calvin's Case* in 2 BACON, WORKS 176. See also HALE, HISTORY OF THE COMMON LAW (1779) § 13: "Of the **Rights** of the People or Subject," where it is said these are protected according to their "lives, their liberties, their estates."

[61] Foster, *International Calvinism through John Locke and the Revolution of 1688* (1927) 32 AM. HIST. REV. 475.

analogy to anything in Locke; and the doctrine of election with its undemocratic implications is entirely antithetical to Lockian optimism.[62] The founder of the Geneva theocracy, who burned Servetus at the stake, and the author of the *Letters on Toleration* have little in common.

It is evident that certain important distinctions have been overlooked. The entire Protestant movement with its emphasis on the priesthood of the individual believer was permeated with individualistic implications; but before these could come to effective political expression, they had to be released from the very medievalism which Calvinism seems at the outset to have been principally bent on restoring.[63] Fortunately for its ultimate reputation in the history of political thought, Calvinism found itself much more frequently than not in the position of a religious minority subject to persecution. Its adherents were consequently forced either to adopt Calvin's own teaching of non-resistance, or to develop a type of political theory that countenanced resistance, and many of them took the latter route. That is to say, because of the actual situation of Calvinism, certain Calvinists developed doctrines of political liberalism, as for that matter did also certain Catholic writers of the

[62] 2 DUNNING, *op. cit. supra* note 60, at 26 *et seq.*; 2 MACKINNON, HISTORY OF MODERN LIBERTY (1906) 147–53. "It is, however, the disciples of Calvin, rather than the master himself, who advanced the theory of resistance, and Calvin's attitude was more authoritarian than that of Luther. Luther's intolerance was merely that of an enthusiast, Calvin's was that of a strong ruler, who dislikes all obstacles in the way of a uniform system. Calvin's bigotry was that of a lawyer or an inquisitor, Luther's that of a preacher or a schoolboy." FIGGIS, GERSON TO GROTIUS (1916) 138. Calvinism "certainly did not favour individual liberty; but it was opposed in theory to secular interference, and by its own methods to monarchical power. Hence in spite of itself Calvinism in France, in the Netherlands and Scotland became either in the world of thought or in that of practice the basis of modern liberty." *Ibid.* 155–56. Calvin's chief service to liberty, by way of theory, was shunting "sovereignty" off to heaven. This helped to keep the ground clear for popular sovereignty once the theocrats were disposed of. The Jesuits, operating from different premises, performed a similar service by emphasizing the secular character of political authority.

[63] FIGGIS, *op. cit. supra* note 62, at 21–22.

same era.[64] As Dr. Figgis has put it, "Political liberty is the residuary legatee of ecclesiastical animosities." [65]

Nor is this to disparage Locke's indebtedness to such forerunners, which was indeed immense. For taking up the thread of later medieval political thought at the point where it had been broken off by Machiavelli and Bodin, to say nothing of Luther and Calvin, they at once revived the postulates of popular sovereignty which underlay Roman law and institutions and supplemented these by principles adapted from the matured Roman law of private contract.[66] Yet, this concession made, it still remains true that the contact of Locke's system with the writers alluded to is indirect, and through a question which they left unsolved rather than through those they purported to answer. Sixteenth century liberalism rested its case largely on the notion of an original compact between governors and governed, between rulers and the people.[67] The question inevitably emerged: Who are "the people," and how did they become an entity capable of contracting?

Locke's own answer to these questions springs from a threefold rootage. Its primary source was English legal tradition as illustrated in Fortescue and Coke, the entire emphasis of which has always been on rights of the individual rather than on rights of the people considered in the mass.[68] The latter, indeed, was sufficiently provided for in Parliament. A second source was English Independency, which was in turn the direct outgrowth of Luther's doctrine of the priesthood of the individual. For in a period in which religious and political controversy were so closely involved with each other as in seventeenth century England, ideas developed in the one forum were easily

[64] 2 Dunning, *op. cit. supra* note 60, at 67 *et seq.,* also c. 4.

[65] Figgis, *op. cit. supra* note 62, at 118.

[66] 2 Dunning, *op. cit. supra* note 60, at c. 2; Gooch, English Democratic Ideas in the Seventeenth Century (1898) Intro. and c. 1. On the doctrine of popular sovereignty in the later Middle Ages, see Gierke, Althusius 69 and n.36; Gierke, Political Theories of the Middle Ages (Maitland tr. 1922) 37–40; Figgis, *op. cit. supra* note 62, at c. 2.

[67] 2 Dunning, *op. cit. supra* note 60, at 79.

[68] See page 37, *supra,* for Fortescue's anticipation of Locke.

and inevitably transferred to the other. Finally, Locke himself would have been the first to own his indebtedness to Grotius and Pufendorf [69] and so ultimately to Cicero; while his citations of "the judicious Hooker," a still earlier apostle of the Ciceronian revival, outnumber those to any other writer. The first and last of these sources need only to be cataloged. The second, however, demands some further comment.

The leader of the extreme sect of the Independents, called the Levellers, was John Lilburne, a veritable ragamuffin, in whose writings the concern of his highly respectable successor, Locke, for "property" is replaced by demands for the "natural rights" of freedom of conscience and expression, and to political equality [70]—demands which even in the deepest dungeons he seems never to have lacked pen and ink to indite. The political *chef d'oeuvre* of Independency was the famous Agreement of the People of 1647, which was an effort to give concrete realization to the principle of the Social Compact.[71]

In America the filiation of Independency with the Social Compact philosophy can be traced at a still earlier date in connection with the Pilgrim foundation of Plymouth. The expedition comprised John Robinson's Scrooby congregation, of which a contemporary critic wrote: "Do we not know the beginnings of his Church? that there was first one stood up and made a covenant, and then another, and these two joyned together, and so a third, and these became a church, say they." [72]

[69] "When a young Gentleman has pretty well digested *Tully's Offices* and added to it *Puffendorff de Officio Hominis & Civis,* it may be seasonable to set him upon *Grotius de Jure Belli & Pacis;* or, which perhaps is the better of the two, *Puffendorff de Jure naturali & Gentium;* wherein he will be instructed in the natural Rights of man and the Originals and Foundations of Society and Duties resulting from thence. . . ." 3 LOCKE, WORKS (1823) 84, quoted in the introduction to FORTESCUE, DE LAUDIBUS LEGUM ANGLIAE (Gregor ed. 1775) xx.

[70] 2 DUNNING, *op. cit. supra note* 60, at 234 *et seq.;* GOOCH, *op. cit. supra note* 60, at 141–46, 200–03, 253–56; PEASE, THE LEVELLER MOVEMENT (1916) *passim.*

[71] 2 DUNNING, *op. cit. supra* note 60, at 238. The agreement was greatly modified in 1648 and further so in 1649.

[72] DAVIS, JOHN ROBINSON (1903) 48.

And the procedure which, under the sanction of God, was effective to produce a church, could also be availed of under the same sanction to produce a commonwealth, as was shown in the famous Mayflower Compact:

> In the name of God, Amen. We whose names are underwritten, the loyall subjects of our dread soveraigne lord, King James . . . doe by these presents solemnly and mutualy in the presence of God, and one of another, covenant and combine oursselves togeather into a civill body politick, for our better ordering and preservation . . . and by vertue hearof to enacte, constitute, and frame such just and equall lawes, ordinances, acts, constitutions, and offices, from time to time, as shall be thought most meete and convenient for the general good of the Colonie, unto which we promise all due submission and obedience.[73]

Thus, more than two generations before Locke's *Second Treatise,* a social compact was conceived as supplying the second permanent government within what is now the United States. Whereas with Locke the ultimate basis of authority is supplied by natural law, here it is supplied by God. We shall observe presently how the rapprochement between the two positions was effected by eighteenth century Deism.

A generation later, though still more than a generation before the appearance of Locke's *Treatise,* we find another Independent, Thomas Hooker of Connecticut, proffering the theory of contract as explanatory of all human association.

> Every spiritual or ecclesiastical corporation receives its being from a spiritual combination . . . there is no man constrained to enter into such a condition, unless he will; and he that will enter, must also willingly bind and engage himself to each member of that society to promote the good of the whole, or else a member actually he is not.[74]

Though Hooker is here speaking of "ecclesiastical corporations," the Fundamental Orders of Connecticut of 1639,

[73] MacDonald, Documentary Source Book of American History (1920) 19.

[74] Walker, Life of Thomas Hooker (1891) 124–25. I am indebted for this and the reference in note 72, to my friend, Professor W. S. Carpenter.

whereby the inhabitants of the three towns did "assotiate and conjoyne" themselves "to be as one Publike State or Common-welth," embodies his political application of the same thought.[75] Nor is this the only significance of the Fundamental Orders. Taken along with the Agreement of the People a decade later, it shows the powerful, ineluctable necessity felt by those who held the compact theory for placing governmental institutions on a documentary basis.

One other predecessor of Locke must be mentioned before turning more particularly to the *Second Treatise,* Thomas Hobbes, author of the *Leviathan.* It is usual to contrast these two writers, but they also have much in common, and in relation to American constitutional theory, their contributions are often complementary rather than contradictory. For if Locke shares with Coke the paternity of American constitutional limitations, Hobbes's emphasis upon the *salus populi* is a definite forerunner of the modern doctrine of the police power, as well as a clear prophecy of legal tendency even in a constitutional state when conditions of emergency menace public order. Hobbes is at the outset as thoroughly individualistic as Locke, and the prosecution by the individual of his own interest is as much his objective as it is Locke's. Both Hobbes and Locke also agree in dispensing with the governmental contract; but whereas a sovereign law-making body is the direct outcome of the social compact with Hobbes, with Locke it is the corporate majority, which then determines the form of government.

Where Hobbes and Locke part company is in their view of the state of nature, that is to say, in their view of human nature when not subjected to political control. Hobbes, a timid man who had been called upon to witness stern events, pictures the state of nature as one of "force and fraud," in which "every man is to every man a wolf." [76] Locke, who was perhaps of a more robust type, and at any rate wrote amid happier surroundings, depicts the state of nature as in the main an era of "peace, good will, mutual assistance, and preservation," in

[75] MacDonald, *op. cit. supra* note 73, at 36–39.
[76] Hobbes, Leviathan (1651) c. 13.

which the "free, sovereign" individual is already in possession of all valuable rights, though from defect of "executive power" he is not always able to make them good or to determine them accurately in relation to the like rights of his fellows.[77] And from this difference flow all the others. With Hobbes a dissolution of government is substantially a dissolution of society; with Locke it is not, society having existed before government. With Hobbes natural law and civil law are coextensive; that is to say, "when a commonwealth is once settled, then are they [natural laws] actually laws, and not before." [78] With Locke, natural law approximates to positive law from the first, while even after the establishment of government, popular interpretation of natural law is the ultimate test of the validity of civil law. Thus Hobbes becomes, more or less in spite of himself, the founder of the Positive School of Jurisprudence, which traces all rights to government and regards them simply as implements of public policy. Locke, on the other hand, regards government as creative of no rights, but as strictly fiduciary in character, and as designed to make more secure and more readily available rights which antedate it and which would survive it.

The two features of the *Second Treatise* which have impressed themselves most definitely upon American constitutional law are the limitations which it lays down for legislative power and its emphasis on the property right. The legislature

[77] LOCKE, SECOND TREATISE ON CIVIL GOVERNMENT (Everyman's ed. 1924) c. 2, 118.

[78] HOBBES, LEVIATHAN c. 26. " 'Civil law,' is to every subject, those rules, which the commonwealth hath commanded him, by word, writing, or other sufficient sign of the will, to make use of, for the distinction of right and wrong; that is to say, of what is contrary and what is not contrary to the rule." *Ibid*. c. 26. In the face of this definition of "right," Hobbes, in order to base his commonwealth on contract, asserts that "when a covenant is made, then to break it is 'unjust'; and the definition of 'injustice' is no other than 'the not performance of covenant.' " *Ibid*. c. 15. Nor does Locke escape a contradiction of a different sort. The SECOND TREATISE ON CIVIL GOVERNMENT is founded on conceptions not drawn from experience, whereas the object of the ESSAY CONCERNING HUMAN UNDERSTANDING is to discredit such ideas. 1 STEPHEN, HORAE SABBATICAE (1892) 150 in Carpenter, *Introduction* to LOCKE, *op. cit. supra* note 77, at xvii.

is the supreme organ of Locke's commonwealth, and it is upon this supremacy that he depends in the main for the safeguarding of the rights of the individual. But for this very reason legislative supremacy is supremacy within the law, not a power above the law. In fact, the word "sovereign" is never used by Locke in its descriptive sense except in reference to the "free, sovereign" individual in the state of nature. In detail, the limitations which Locke specifies to legislative power are the following: [79] First, it is not arbitrary power. Not even the majority which determines the form of the government can vest its agent with arbitrary power, for the reason that the majority right itself originates in a delegation by free sovereign individuals who had "in the state of nature no arbitrary power over the life, liberty, or possessions" of others, or even over their own. In this caveat against "arbitrary power," Locke definitely anticipates the modern latitudinarian concept of due process of law.

"Secondly, the legislative . . . cannot assume to itself a power to rule by extemporary, arbitrary decrees, but is bound to dispense justice and decide the rights of the subject by promulgated standing laws, and known authorised judges"; nor may it vary the law in particular cases, but there must be one rule for rich and poor, for favorite and the ploughman. In this pregnant passage, Locke foreshadows some of the most fundamental propositions of American constitutional law: *Law must be general; it must afford equal protection to all; it may not validly operate retroactively; it must be enforced through the courts—legislative power does not include judicial power.*

Thirdly, as also follows from its fiduciary character, the legislature "cannot transfer the power of making laws to any other hands: for it being but a delegated power from the people, they who have it cannot pass it over to others." More briefly, *legislative power cannot be delegated.*

Finally, *legislative power is not the ultimate power of the commonwealth,* for "the community perpetually retains a supreme power of saving themselves from the attempts and de-

[79] *Of the Extent of the Legislative Power* in LOCKE, *op. cit. supra* note 77, at c. 11, 183 *et seq.*

signs of anybody, even their legislators, whenever they shall be so foolish or so wicked as to lay and carry on designs against the liberties and properties of the subject." So while legislative supremacy is the normal sanction of the rights of men, it is not the final sanction. The identical power which was exerted against James II would in like case be equally available against Parliament itself.[80]

Locke's bias in favor of property is best shown in the fifth chapter of the *Treatise,* where he brings the labor theory of value to the defense of inequality of possessions, and endeavors to show that the latter is harmonious with the social compact. His course of reasoning is as follows: All value, or almost all, is due to labor; and as there were different degrees of industry, so there were apt to be different degrees of possession. Yet most property, in those early days, was highly perishable, whence arose a natural limit to the accumulation of wealth, to wit, that no man must hoard up more than he could make use of, since that would be to waste nature's bounty. Nevertheless, "the exceeding of his just property" lay, Locke is careful to insist, not "in the largeness of his possession, but the perishing of anything uselessly in it." Accordingly, when mankind, by affixing value to gold, silver, and other imperishable but intrinsically valueless things for which perishable commodities might be traded, made exchanges possible, it thereby, as by deliberate consent, ratified unequal possessions; and the later social compact did not disturb this covenant.[81]

So, having transmuted the law of nature into the rights of men, Locke next converts these into the rights of ownership. The final result is to base his commonwealth upon the bal-

[80] LOCKE, *op. cit. supra* note 77, at c. 19, 224.

[81] *Of Property, ibid.* c. 5, 129. Locke uses the term "property" with various degrees of precision. In chapter 5 he is thinking of *things* with exchangeable value. In chapter 7 he uses the word to cover "life, liberty, and estate." In *A Letter on Toleration* he says that the commonwealth exists to promote "civil interest," and "civil interest I call life, liberty, inviolability of Body, and the possession of such outward things as Money, Lands, Houses, Furniture, and the like." 2 LOCKE, WORKS (1823) 239, quoted by LASKI, GRAMMAR OF POLITICS (1925) 181.

anced and antithetical concepts of the rule of the majority and the security of property. Nor, thanks to the labor theory of value, is this the merely static conception that at first consideration it might seem to be. Taken up a century later by Adam Smith, the labor theory became the cornerstone of the doctrine of *laissez faire*.[82] It thus assisted to adapt a political theory conceived in the interest of a quiescent landed aristocracy to the uses of an aggressive industrial plutocracy. By the same token, it also assisted to adapt a theory conceived for a wealthy and civilized community to the exactly opposed conditions of life in a new and undeveloped country. In a frontier society engrossed in the conquest of nature and provided with but meagre stimulation to artistic and intellectual achievement, the inevitable index of success was accumulation, and accumulation did, in fact, represent social service. What is more, the singular affinity which Calvinistic New England early discovered for Lockian rationalism is in some measure explicable on like grounds. The central pillar of Calvinism was the doctrine of election. It goes without saying that all who believed this dogma also believed themselves among the elect; yet of this what better, what more objective evidence than material success? Locke himself, it may be added, was a notable preacher of the gospel of industry and thrift.[83]

---

[82] CAREY, HARMONY OF INTERESTS, AGRICULTURAL, MANUFACTURING AND COMMERCIAL (1872). Henry C. Carey attempts an application of Smith's theory to American conditions in favor of a protective tariff.

[83] Foster, *supra* note 61, at 486. See also ROBINSON, CASE OF LOUIS THE ELEVENTH AND OTHER ESSAYS (1928); Weber, *Protestantische Ethick u. der "Geist" des Kapitalismus* (1904) 30 ARCHIV FÜR SOZIAL-WISSENSCHAFT U. SOZIAL POLITIK 1–54; (1905) 21 *id.* 1–110; SOMBART, QUINTESSENCE OF CAPITALISM (1915) 257–62; and Tawney, *Puritanism and Capitalism* (1926) 46 NEW REPUBLIC 348. Puritanism has been not inaptly characterized as "a religious sublimation of the virtues of the middle class." Puritan abhorrence of beauty and amusement necessarily led to concentration on the business of money-getting; and the belief of the Puritans that they were "chosen people" worked to the same end, for it turned their attention to the Old Testament, where the idea that prosperity is proof of moral worth is repeatedly presented. Nor is the New Testament devoid of such ideas. Compare the parable of the Talents, MATTHEW xxv, 29; also ROMANS xii, 11;

Two other features of Locke's thought deserve brief comment. The first is his insistence upon the "public good" as the object of legislation and of governmental action in general. It should not be supposed that this in any way contradicts the main trend of his thought. Rather he is laying down yet another limitation on legislative freedom of action.[84] That the public good might not always be compatible with the preservation of rights, and especially with the rights of property, never once occurs to him. A century later the possibility did occur to Adam Smith, and was waived aside by his "harmony of interests" theory. Also the dimensions which Locke assigns to executive prerogative are, in view both of the immediate occasion for which he wrote and of his "constitutionalism," not a little astonishing. On this matter he writes:

Where the legislative and executive power are in distinct hands (as they are in all moderated monarchies and well-framed governments), there the good of the society requires, that several things should be left to the discretion of him that has the executive power: for the legislators not being able to foresee, and provide by laws, for all that may be useful to the community, the executor of the laws, having the power in his hands, has by the common law of nature a right to make use of it for the good of the society, in many cases, where the municipal law has given no direction, till the legislative can conveniently be assembled to provide for it; Many things there are, which the law can by no means provide for; and those must necessarily be left to the discretion of him that has the executive power in his hands, to be ordered by him as the public good and advantage shall require: nay, it is fit that the laws themselves should in some cases give way to the executive power, or rather to the fundamental law of nature and government—viz., That as much as may be, all the members of the society are to be preserved.[85]

---

and see especially the texts from BAXTER, CHRISTIAN DIRECTORY, quoted by ROBINSON, *loc. cit. supra*.

[84] "Their [the legislature's] power, in the utmost bounds of it, is limited to the public good of the society." LOCKE, SECOND TREATISE ON CIVIL GOVERNMENT C. 11, § 135; *cf.* §§ 89, 110, 134, 142, 158 with §§ 124, 131, 140.

[85] LOCKE, *op. cit. supra* note 84, "Of Prerogative," c. 14, § 159.

Extrication from the trammels of a too rigid constitutionalism through a broad view of executive power is a device by no means unknown to American constitutional law and theory.

Locke's contribution is best estimated in relation to Coke's. Locke's version of natural law not only rescues Coke's version of the English constitution from a localized *patois,* restating it in the universal tongue of the age, it also supplements it in important respects. Coke's endeavor was to put forward the historical procedure of the common law as a permanent restraint on power, and especially on the power of the English crown. Locke, in the limitations which he imposes on legislative power, is looking rather to the security of the substantive rights of the individual—those rights which are implied in the basic arrangements of society at all times and in all places. While Coke rescued the notion of fundamental law from what must sooner or later have proved a fatal nebulosity, yet he did so at the expense of archaism. Locke, on the other hand, in cutting loose in great measure from the historical method of reasoning, opened the way to the larger issues with which American constitutional law has been called upon to grapple in its latest maturity. Without the Lockian or some similar background, judicial review must have atrophied by 1890 in the very field in which it is today most active; nor is this to forget his emphasis on the property right. Locke's weakness is on the institutional side. While he contributed to the *doctrine* of judicial review, it was without intention; nor does he reveal any perception of the importance of giving imperative written form to the constitutional principles which he formulated. The hardfisted Coke, writing with a civil war ahead of him instead of behind him, was more prescient.

[V]

The influence of higher law doctrine associated with the names of Coke and Locke was at its height in England during the period when the American colonies were being most actively settled, which means that Coke had, to begin with, the advantage since he was first on the ground. The presence of

Coke's doctrines in the colonies during the latter two-thirds of the seventeenth century is widely evidenced by the repeated efforts of colonial legislatures to secure for their constituencies the benefits of *Magna Carta* and particularly of the twenty-ninth chapter thereof. Because of the menace they were thought to spell for the prerogative, the majority of such measures incurred the royal veto.[86] In point of fact, since the "law of the land" clause of chapter twenty-nine was interpretable as contemplating only law which was enacted by the colonial legislature, the menace when even further. Clothed with this construction, chapter twenty-nine afforded affirmation not only of rights of the individual, but also of local legislative autonomy.[87] The frequently provoked discussion of such matters, moreover, served to fix terminology for the future moulding of thought. *Magna Carta* became a generic term for all documents of constitutional significance, and thereby a symbol and reminder of principles binding on government.[88]

But more specific evidence of Coke's influence also occurs during this period. One such instance is furnished by the opinion of a Massachusetts magistrate in 1657 holding void a tax by the town of Ipswich for the purpose of presenting the local minister with a dwelling house. Such a tax, said the magistrate, "to take from Peter and give it to Paul," is against fundamental law. "If noe kinge or Parliament can justly enact or cause that one man's estate, in whole or in part, may be taken from him and given to another without his owne consent, then surely the major part of a towne or other inferior powers cannot doe it." [89] An opinion of the attorney general of the Barbados, rendered sometime during the reign of Anne, which held void a paper money act because it authorized summary process against debtors, is of like import. The entire argument is based on chapter twenty-nine of *Magna Carta* and "common right, or

[86] For details, see HAZELTINE, MAGNA CARTA COMMEMORATION ESSAYS (1917) 191–201. MOTT, DUE PROCESS OF LAW (1926) cc. 1, 6, adds some further items.

[87] HAZELTINE, *loc. cit. supra* note 86, at 195.   [88] *Ibid.* 199–200.

[89] 2 HUTCHINSON, PAPERS (Prince Soc. Pubs. 1865) 1–25.

reason." [90] Evidence of the persistence of the dictum in *Bonham's Case* also crops up outside New England now and then, even before its notable revival by Otis in his argument in the *Writs of Assistance Case*.[91] As late as 1759 we find a New York man referring quite incidentally to "a Judicial power of declaring them [laws] void." [92] The allusion is inexplicable unless it was to Coke's "dictum."

If the seventeenth century was Coke's, the early half of the eighteenth was Locke's, especially in New England. After the Glorious Revolution the migration to America of important English elements ceased. Immediate touch with political developments in the mother country was thus lost. The colonies were fain henceforth to be content for the most part with the stock of political ideas already on hand; and in fact these met their own necessities, which grew chiefly out of the quarrels between the governors and the assemblies, extremely well. And along with this comparative isolation from new currents of thought in the mother country went the general intellectual poverty of frontier life itself. There were few books, fewer newspapers, and little travel. But one source of intellectual stimulation for the adult there was, one point of contact with the world of ideas, and that was the sermon. Through their election sermons in particular and through controversial pamphlets, the New England clergy taught their flocks political theory, and almost always this was an elaboration upon the stock of ideas which had come from seventeenth century England. The subject has been so admirably treated in a recent volume that it is here necessary only to record some of the outstanding facts.[93]

After the Bible, Locke was the principal authority relied on by the preachers to bolster up their political teachings, although Coke, Pufendorf, Sydney, and later on some others were

[90] 2 CHALMERS, OPINIONS OF EMINENT LAWYERS (1814) 27–38, especially at 30.

[91] See MOTT, DUE PROCESS OF LAW 91, n.19.

[92] 2 NEW YORK HISTORICAL SOCIETY COLLECTIONS (1869) 204.

[93] BALDWIN, THE NEW ENGLAND CLERGY AND THE AMERICAN REVOLUTION ⟨1928⟩.

also cited. The substance of the doctrine of these discourses is, except at two points, that of the *Second Treatise*. Natural rights and the social compact, government bounded by law and incapable of imparting legality to measures contrary to law, and the right of resistance to illegal measures all fall into their proper place. One frequent point of deviation from the Lockian model is the retention of the idea of a compact between governed and governors; that notion fitted in too well with the effort to utilize the colonial charters as muniments of local liberty to be discarded.[94] The other point of deviation from Locke is more apparent than real, for all these concepts are backed up by religious sanction. Yet to the modern reader the difference between the Puritan God of the eighteenth century and Locke's natural law often seems little more than nominal. "The Voice of Nature is the Voice of God," asserts one preacher; "reason and the voice of God are one," is the language of another; "Christ confirms the law of nature," is the teaching of a third.[95] The point of view is thoroughly deistic; reason has usurped the place of revelation, and without affront to piety.

Nor should it be imagined that all this teaching and preaching on political topics took place *in vacuo*—in deliberate preparation, as it were, for a great emergency as yet descried only by the most perspicacious. Much of it was evoked by warm and bitter controversy among the New England congregations themselves.[96] One such controversy was that which arose in the second decade of the eighteenth century over the question whether the congregations should submit themselves to the governance of a synod. Even more heated was the quarrel which was produced by the great awakening consequent on the preaching of George Whitefield in 1740. Whitefield's doctrine was distinctly and disturbingly equalitarian. A spirit of criticism of superiors by inferiors, of elders by juniors ensued from it; while, at the

94 The same fact may also account for John Wise's preference for Pufendorf over Locke, though this may be due to his having had a copy of the former and not of the latter.

95 BALDWIN, *op. cit. supra* note 93, 29n., 43, 73n. See also note 57, *supra*.

96 *Ibid.* cc. 5–6.

same time the intellectual superiority of the clergy was menaced by the sudden appearance of a great crop of popular exhorters. Men turned again to Locke, Sydney, and others, but this time in order to discover the sanctions of authority rather than its limitations. Still some years later the outbreak of the French and Indian Wars inspired a series of sermons extolling English liberty and contrasting the balanced constitution of England with French tyranny, sermons in which the name of Montesquieu was now joined with that of Locke.[97]

This kind of preaching was not confined to New England, nor even to dissenting clergymen. Patrick Henry from his eleventh to his twenty-second year listened to an Anglican preacher who taught that the British constitution was but the "voluntary compact of sovereign and subject." Henry's own words later were "government is a conditional compact between king and people . . . violation of the covenant by either party discharges the other from obligation"; [98] and more than half of the signers of the Declaration of Independence were members of the Church of England.[99] It is also an important circumstance that the famous Parson's Cause, in which Henry participated as the champion of local liberty, was pending in Virginia from 1752 to 1758, helping to bring the people of Virginia during the period face to face with fundamental constitutional questions.[100] "On a small scale, the whole episode illustrates the clash of political theories which lay back of the American Revolution." [101] And meantime the first generation of the American bar was coming to maturity—students of Coke, and equipped

[97] *Ibid.* 88–89.

[98] Van Tyne, *Influence of the Clergy on the American Revolution* (1913) 14 Am. Hist. Rev. 49.

[99] Letter of G. MacLaren Brydon, *N. Y. Times,* May 30, 1927, citing Perry, The Faith of the Signers of the Declaration of Independence (1926). All the signers from the Southern Colonies except one from Maryland (a Catholic) and one from Georgia were Anglicans.

[100] Scott, *The Constitutional Aspects of the "Parson's Cause"* (1916) 31 Pol. Sci. Q. 558 *et seq.* The controversy evoked much talk of "void laws," though from the clerical party and with reference to acts of the Virginia Assembly.

[101] *Ibid.* 577.

to bring his doctrines to the support of Locke should the need arise.[102]

The opening gun of the controversy leading to the Revolution was Otis' argument in 1761 in the *Writs of Assistance Case*,[103] which, through Bacon's and Viner's *Abridgments,* goes straight back to *Bonham's Case.* Adams' summary of it reads: "As to acts of Parliament. An act against the Constitution is void: an Act against natural Equity is void: and if an Act of Parliament should be made, in the very words of the petition, it would be void. The Executive Courts must pass such Acts into disuse.—8 Rep. 118 from Viner." [104] "Then and there," exclaims Adams, "the child Independence was born." [105] Today he must have added that then and there American constitutional law was born, for Otis' contention goes far beyond Coke's: an ordinary court may traverse the specifically enacted will of Parliament, and its condemnation is final.

The suggestion that the local courts might be thus pitted against an usurping Parliament in defence of "British rights," served to bring the idea of judicial review to the very threshold of the first American constitutions, albeit it was destined to wait there unattended for some years. Adams himself in a plea before the Governor and Council of Massachusetts, turned Otis' argument against the Stamp Act,[106] while a Virginia county court actually declared that measure void. "The judges were

[102] WARREN, HISTORY OF THE AMERICAN BAR (1911) cc. 2–8; LECKY, AMERICAN REVOLUTION (Woodburn ed. 1922) 15–16.

[103] Quincy (Mass. 1761) 51–57, and appendices, 395–552, of which 469–85 are especially relevant; also 2 ADAMS, LIFE AND WORKS (C. F. Adams ed. 1850) 521–25, and 10 *ibid.* 232–362 *passim.*

[104] Quincy 474 (Mass. 1761).   [105] 10 ADAMS, LIFE AND WORKS 248.

[106] 2 *ibid.* 158–59; Memorial of Boston, Quincy 200–02 (Mass. 1765). Otis also spoke to the same effect. *Ibid.* at 205. Adams reiterated his argument in *Letters of Clarendon* in 3 ADAMS, WORKS 469. An argument greatly stressed against the Stamp Act was its tendency to abolish trial by jury contrary to Magna Charta, through its extension of the jurisdiction of the admiralty courts, over penalties incurred under the act. *Ibid.* at 470. Governor Hutchinson wrote at this period: "The prevailing reason at this time is, that the Act of Parliament is against Magna Charta, and the natural Rights of Englishmen, and therefore, according to Lord Coke, null and void." Appendix, Quincy 527n. (Mass. 1769); and to same effect, *ibid.* at 441, 445.

unanimously of the opinion," a report of the case reads, "that the law did not bind, affect, or concern the inhabitants of Virginia 'inasmuch as they conceived the said act to be unconstitutional.' " [107] As late as 1776, Chief Justice William Cushing of Massachusetts, who was later one of Washington's first appointees to the Supreme Court of the United States, was congratulated by Adams for telling a jury of the nullity of acts of Parliament.[108]

Nor did the controversy with Great Britain long rest purely on Coke's doctrines. Otis himself, declares Adams, "was also a great master of the law of nature and nations. He had read Pufendorf, Grotius, Barbeyrac, Burlamaqui, Vattel, Heineccius. . . . It was a maxim which he inculcated in his pupils . . . that a lawyer ought never to be without a volume of natural or public law, or moral philosophy, on his table or in his pocket." [109] Otis' own pamphlet, *The Rights of the British Colonies Asserted and Proved,* none the less was almost altogether of Lockian provenience. The colonists were entitled to "as ample rights, liberties, and privileges as the subjects of the mother country are and in some respects to more. . . . Should the charter privileges of the Colonists be disregarded or revoked, there are natural, inherent, and inseparable rights as men and citizens that would remain." [110] And Adams argues the year following in his dissertation on *The Canon and the Feudal Law for*

---

[107] 5 McMaster, History of the American People (1920) 394.

[108] 9 Adams, Life and Works 390. Meanwhile, the dictum, with a strong Lockian infusion, had been invoked against domestic legislation. See George Mason's argument in Robin v. Hardaway, Jefferson 109–23 (Va. 1772), in which an act of the Virginia Assembly, passed in 1682, was declared void. Mason relied mainly on Coke and Hobart.

[109] 10 Adams, Life and Works 275.

[110] The date of the pamphlet is 1764. A summary of it in 10 Adams, Life and Works 293, is a summary of Locke's eleventh chapter. In Otis, Vindication of the House of Representatives (1762), Locke is characterized as "one of the most wise . . . most honest . . . most impartial men that ever lived . . . as great an ornament . . . the Church of England ever had to boast of."

Rights antecedent to all earthly government—Rights that cannot be repealed or restrained by human laws—Rights derived from the great Legislator of the universe. . . . British liberties are not the grants of princes or parliaments, but original rights, conditions of original contracts . . . coeval with government. . . . Many of our rights are inherent and essential, agreed on as maxims, and established as preliminaries, even before a parliament existed.[111]

But it is the Massachusetts Circular Letter of 1768 that perfects the blend of Coke and Locke, while it also reformulates in striking terms, borrowed perhaps from Vattel, the medieval notion of authority as intrinsically conditioned. The outstanding paragraph of the letter is the following:

The House have humbly represented to the ministry, their own sentiments, that his Majesty's high court of Parliament is the supreme legislative power over the whole empire; that in all free states the constitution is fixed, and as the supreme legislative derives its power and authority from the constitution, it cannot overleap the bounds of it, without destroying its own foundation; that the constitution ascertains and limits both sovereignty and allegiance, and, therefore, his Majesty's American subjects, who acknowledge themselves bound by the ties of allegiance, have an equitable claim to the full enjoyment of the fundamental rules of the British constitution; that it is an essential, unalterable right, in nature, engrafted into the British constitution, as a fundamental law, and ever held sacred and irrevocable by the subjects within the realm, that what a man has honestly acquired is absolutely his own, which he may freely give, but cannot be taken from him without his consent; that the American subjects may, therefore, exclusive of any consideration of charter rights, with a decent firmness, adopted to the character of free men and subjects, assert this natural and constitutional right.[112]

Notwithstanding all this, as late as the first Continental Congress there were still those who opposed any reliance whatsoever on natural rights. One of "the two points which we la-

111 3 ADAMS, LIFE AND WORKS 448–64, especially at 449, 463.

112 MacDONALD, DOCUMENTARY SOURCE BOOK 146–50. *Cf.* VATTEL, LAW OF NATIONS (London tr. 1797) bk. i, c. 3, § 34. The subordination of the legislative authority and that of the Prince to the constitution is the gospel of this and the succeeding chapter. The work first appeared in 1758.

boured most" John Adams records in his *Diary* was "whether we should recur to the law of nature, as well as to the British constitution, and our American charters and grants. Mr. Galloway and Mr. Duane were for excluding the law of nature. I was strenuous for retaining and insisting on it, as a recourse to which we might be driven by Parliament much sooner than we were aware." [113] The "Declaration and Resolves" of the Congress proves that Adams carried the day. The opening resolution asserts "that the inhabitants of the American colonies in North America," by the immutable laws of nature, the principles of the British constitution, and the several charters or compacts "are entitled to life, liberty, and property." [114]

Nor did the corollary notion of a single community claiming common rights on the score of a common humanity, escape American spokesmen. It was in this same first Continental Congress that Patrick Henry made his famous deliverance:

Government is dissolved. . . . Where are your landmarks, your boundaries of Colonies? We are in a state of nature, sir. . . . The distinctions between Virginians, Pennsylvanians, New Yorkers, and New Englanders, are no more. I am not a Virginian, but an American.[115]

And the less casual evidence of everyday speech is to like effect: "the people of these United Colonies," "your whole people," "the people of America," "the liberties of Americans," "the rights of Americans," "American rights," "Americans." [116] The constant recurrence of such phrases in contemporary documents bespeaks the conscious identity of Americans everywhere in possession of the rights of men. Natural rights were already on the way to become national rights.

At the same time it is necessary to recognize that the Ameri-

[113] ADAMS, LIFE AND WORKS 374.

[114] MacDONALD, *op. cit. supra* note 112, at 162–66.

[115] 2 ADAMS, LIFE AND WORKS 366–67.

[116] BALDWIN, VIEW OF THE ORIGIN AND NATURE OF THE CONSTITUTION OF THE UNITED STATES (1837) 15–16; DILLON, LAWS AND JURISPRUDENCE OF ENGLAND AND AMERICA (1895) 46–48. See also NILES, PRINCIPLES AND ACTS (1876) 134–35, 148.

can Revolution was also a contest for local autonomy as well as one for individual liberty. The two motives were in fact less competitive than complementary. The logical deduction from the course of political history in the colonies, especially in the later decades of it, was that the best protection of the rights of the individual was to be found in the maintenance of the hard-won prerogatives of the colonial legislatures against the royal governors; in other words, of what they locally termed their "Constitutions." [117] The final form of the American argument against British pretentions was, therefore, by no means a happy idea suggested by the stress of contention, but was soundly based on autochthonous institutional developments. As stated by Jefferson in his *Summary View,* published in 1774, it comprised the thesis that Parliament had no power whatsoever to legislate for the colonies, whether in harmony with the rights of men or no; that the colonies were mutually independent communities, equal partners in the British Empire with England herself; that each part had its own parliament which was the supreme law-making power within its territorial limits; that each was connected with the Empire only through the person of a common monarch, who was "no more than the chief officer of the people, appointed by the laws . . . to assist in working the great machine of government erected for their use." [118] The Declaration of Independence, two years later from

[117] For this use of the term "Constitution," sometimes referring to the colonial charter, sometimes referring to the established mode of government of the colony, see 2 JOURNALS OF THE HOUSE OF REPRESENTATIVES OF MASSACHUSETTS (1720) 370; 8 *ibid.* 279, 302, 318 (1728). In New Jersey, which had no charter after 1702, the term "constitution" referred altogether to the mode of government that had developed on the basis of the royal governor's instructions, but may have been suggested by the Fundamental Constitutions of 1683 of East Jersey. C. R. ERDMAN, THE NEW JERSEY CONSTITUTION OF 1776 (to be printed).

[118] 11 JEFFERSON, WRITINGS 258; THE JEFFERSONIAN CYCLOPEDIA (Foley ed. 1900) 963–68. Jefferson characteristically claimed his to be the first formulation of this position. 9 JEFFERSON, WRITINGS 258. But in this he was seriously in error. Richard Bland, Stephen Hopkins, John Adams, James Wilson, Benjamin Franklin, Roger Sherman, James Iredell, and others all preceded him, Hopkins and Franklin by nearly ten years. Indeed, advocates had

the same hand, proceeds on the same theory. It is addressed not to Parliament but to the king, since it was with the king alone that the bond about to be severed had subsisted; in it the American doctrine of the relation of government to individual rights finds its classic expression; these rights are vindicated by the assertion of the independence of the thirteen states.[119]

From the destructive phase of the Revolution we turn to its constructive phase. This time it was Virginia who led the way. The Virginia constitution of 1776 is preceded by a "Declaration of rights made by the representatives of the good people of Virginia . . . which rights do appertain to them and their posterity, as the basis and foundation of government." [120] In this document, antedating the Declaration of Independence by a month, are enumerated at length those rights which Americans, having laid claim to them first as British subjects and later as men, now intended as citizens to secure through governments of their own erection. For the first time in the history of the world the principles of revolution are made the basis of settled political institutions.

What was the nature of these governments? Again the Vir-

---

developed a similar doctrine in Ireland's behalf in the seventeenth century. On the whole subject see ADAMS, POLITICAL IDEAS OF THE AMERICAN REVOLUTION (1922) cc. 3, 5; BECKER, *op. cit. supra* note 56, c. 3; McILWAIN, THE AMERICAN REVOLUTION (1923).

[119] Jefferson's indebtedness to the Virginia Declaration of Rights of 1776 appears more striking when the Declaration of Independence is compared with the former as it came from the hands of George Mason. NILES, PRINCIPLES AND ACTS 301–03. The phrase "pursuit of happiness" was probably suggested by Blackstone's statement that the law of nature boils down to "one paternal precept, 'that man should pursue his own true and substantial happiness.'" 1 BL. COMM. 41. BURLAMAQUI, PRINCIPLES OF NATURAL AND POLITICAL LAW (1859), an English translation of which appeared in 1763 (the work was first published in 1747), teaches the same doctrine at length. See, *e.g.*, 2 *ibid.* 18. The phrase "a long train of abuses," is Jefferson's recollection of LOCKE, SECOND TREATISE ON CIVIL GOVERNMENT § 225, c. 19.

[120] 7 THORPE, FEDERAL AND STATE CONSTITUTIONS, COLONIAL CHARTERS AND OTHER ORGANIC LAWS (1909) 3812–14.

ginia constitution of 1776 may serve as a model.[121] Here the horn of the legislative department is mightily exalted, that of the executive correspondingly depressed. The early Virginia governors were chosen by the legislature annually and were assisted by a council of state also chosen by the legislature, and if that body so desired, from the legislature. The governor was without the veto power, or any other participation in the work of law-making, and his salary was entirely at the mercy of the assembly. The judges were in somewhat better case, holding their offices "during good behavior," yet they too were the legislature's appointees, and judicial review is nowhere hinted. Finally, both judges and governors were subject to impeachment, which as still defined by English precedents, amounted to a practically unrestricted inquest of office. The underlying asumption of the instrument, gatherable from its various provisions, is that the rights of the individual have nothing to fear from majority rule exercised through legislative assemblies chosen for brief terms by a restricted, though on the whole democratic, electorate. In short, as in both Coke and Locke, the maintenance of higher law is intrusted to legislative supremacy, though qualified by annual elections. Fortunately or unfortunately, in 1776 the influence of Coke and Locke was no longer the predominant one that it had been. In the very process of controversy with the British Parliament, a new point of view had been brought to American attention, the ultimate consequences of which were as yet unforeseeable.[122]

Lord Acton has described the American Revolution as a contest between two ideas of legislative power. Even as late as the debate on the Declaratory Act of 1766, the American invocation of a constitution setting metes and bounds to Parliament did not fail of a certain response among the English themselves.

[121] *Ibid.* 3814–19.

[122] On the Revolutionary state constitutions, see generally NEVINS, THE AMERICAN STATES DURING AND AFTER THE REVOLUTION (1924); Morey, *First State Constitutions* (1893) 4 ANN. AM. ACAD. POL. AND SOC. SCI. 201–32; Webster, *Comparative Study of the State Constitutions of the American Revolution* (1897) 9 *id.* 380–420.

Burke, it is true, brushed aside all questions of prescriptive rights and based his advocacy of the American cause on expediency only; but Camden, who possessed the greatest legal reputation of the age, quoted both Coke and Locke in support of the proposition that Parliament's power was not an unlimited one; while Chatham, taking halfway ground, pretended to discover a fundamental distinction between the power of taxation and that of legislation, qualifying the former by the necessity of representation.[123] Camden and Chatham were, none the less, illustrious exceptions. The direction which the great weight of professional opinion was now taking was shown when Mansfield, who a few years earlier had as solicitor general quoted the dictum in *Bonham's Case* with approval, arose in the House of Lords to support the Declaratory Act.[124] The passage of that measure by an overwhelming majority committed Parliament substantially to Milton's conclusion of a century earlier that "Parliament was above all positive law, whether civil or common." [125]

The vehicle of the new doctrine to America was Blackstone's

[123] See the debate on the Declaratory Bill, 16 HANSARD, PARLIAMENTARY HISTORY (1813) 163–81, 193–206 *passim*. Camden was especially vehement: The bill is "illegal, absolutely illegal, contrary to the fundamental laws of nature, contrary to the fundamental laws of this constitution." *Ibid.* 178. On the other hand, it was denied that *Magna Carta* was any proof "of our Constitution as it now is. The Constitution of this country has been always in a moving state, either gaining or losing something." *Ibid.* 197.

[124] *Ibid.* 172–75.

[125] McIlwain, HIGH COURT OF PARLIAMENT 94. On the rise of the notion of Parliamentary sovereignty, see HOLDSWORTH, SOME LESSONS FROM OUR LEGAL HISTORY (1928) 112–41. The first to assert the supremacy of the King in Parliament over the King out of Parliament was James Whitlocke, in the debate on Impositions, in 1610. *Ibid.* 124. A division on the subject is shown in the debate on the Septennial Act of 1716. *Ibid.* 129; 7 HANSARD, PARLIAMENTARY HISTORY 317, 334, 339, 348–49. The doctrine of the Declaratory Act evoked numerous protests outside of Parliament. MOTT, DUE PROCESS OF LAW 63n. For a belated expression of the doctrine of limited parliamentary power, see *ibid.* 67n., citing various works of Toulmin Smith. Smith, however, was no advocate of judicial review, but warned his people against such an institution as the Supreme Court of the United States. *Ibid.* 68n.

Commentaries, of which, before the Revolution, nearly 2500 copies had been sold on this side of the Atlantic,[126] while the spread of his influence in the later days of the pre-Revolutionary controversy is testified to by Jefferson in his reference to that "young brood of lawyers" who, seduced by the "honeyed Mansfieldism of Blackstone, . . . began to slide into Toryism." [127] Nor is Blackstone's appeal to men of all parties difficult to understand. Eloquent, suave, undismayed in the presence of the palpable contradictions in his pages, adept in insinuating new points of view without unnecessarily disturbing old ones, he is the very exemplar and model of legalistic and judicial obscurantism.

While still a student, Blackstone had published an essay on *The Absolute Rights of British Subjects,* and chapter one of book one of his greater work bears a like caption. Here he appears at first glance to underwrite the whole of Locke's philosophy, but a closer examination discloses important divergences. "Natural liberty" he defines as "the power of acting as one thinks fit, without any restraint or control, unless by the law of nature." It is "inherent in us by birth," and is that gift of God which corresponds with "the faculty of free will." Yet every man, he continues, "when he enters into society, gives up a part of his natural liberty as the price of so valuable a purchase," receiving in return "civil liberty," which is natural liberty "so far restrained by human laws (and no farther) as is necessary and expedient for the general advantage of the public." [128] The divergence which this phraseology marks from the strictly Lockian position is twofold. Locke also, as we saw above, suggests public utility as one requirement of allowable restraints upon liberty, but by no means the sole requirement;

[126] The first volume appeared in 1765, the fourth in 1769. An American edition appeared in Philadelphia in 1771–72, of the full work, 1400 copies having been ordered in advance. WARREN, HISTORY OF THE AMERICAN BAR 178.

[127] 11 JEFFERSON, WRITINGS (Mem. ed. 1903) iv. Jefferson had no high opinion of "Blackstone lawyers." He termed them "ephemeral insects of the law."

[128] 1 BL. COMM. 125–26.

nor is the law-making power with him, as with Blackstone, the final arbiter of the issue.

The divergence becomes even more evident when the latter turns to consider the positive basis of British liberties in *Magna Carta* and "the corroborating statutes." His language in this connection is peculiarly complacent. The rights declared in these documents, he asserts, comprise nothing less than

either that residuum of natural liberty, which is not required by the laws of society to be sacrificed to public convenience, or else those civil privileges, which society hath engaged to provide in lieu of the natural liberties so given up by individuals. These, therefore, were formerly, either by inheritance or purchase, the rights of all mankind; but, in most other countries of the world, being now more or less debased and destroyed, they at present may be said to remain, in a peculiar and emphatical manner, the rights of the people of England.[129]

Yet when he comes to trace the limits of the "rights and liberties" so grandiloquently characterized, his invariable reference is simply to the state of the law in his own day—never to any more exalted standard.

And so by phraseology drawn from Locke and Coke themselves, he paves the way to the entirely opposed position of Hobbes and Mansfield. In elaboration of this position he lays down the following propositions: First, "there is and must be in all of them [states] a supreme, irresistible, absolute, uncontrolled authority . . ."; secondly, this authority is the "natural, inherent right that belongs to the sovereignty of the state . . . of making and enforcing laws"; thirdly, to the law-making power "all other powers of the state" must conform "in the execution of their several functions or else the Constitution is at an end"; and, finally, the law-making power in Great Britain is Parliament, in which, therefore, the sovereignty resides.[130] It follows, of course, that neither judicial disallowance of acts of Parliament nor yet the right of revolution has either legal or constitutional basis. To be sure, "Acts of Parliament that are

129 *Ibid.* 127–29.   130 *Ibid.* 49–51.

impossible to be performed are of no validity"; yet this is so only in a truistic sense, for "there is no court that has power to defeat the intent of the legislature, when couched in . . . evident and express words." [131] As to the right of revolution—"So long . . . as the English Constitution lasts, we may venture to affirm that the power of Parliament is absolute and without control." [132]

Nor does Blackstone at the end, despite his previous equivocations, flinch from the conclusion that the whole legal fabric of the realm was, by his view, at Parliament's disposal. Thus he writes:

It hath sovereign and uncontrollable authority in the making, confirming, enlarging, restraining, abrogating, repealing, reviving, and expounding of laws . . . this being the place where that absolute, despotic power which must in all governments reside somewhere, is entrusted by the Constitution of these kingdoms. All mischiefs and grievances, operations and remedies that transcend the ordinary course of the laws, are within the reach of this extraordinary tribunal. . . . It can, in short, do everything that is not naturally impossible, and therefore some have not scrupled to call its power by a figure rather too bold, the omnipotence of Parliament. True it is, that what the Parliament doth no authority upon earth can undo.[133]

This absolute doctrine was summed up by De Lolme a little later in the oft-quoted aphorism that "Parliament can do anything except make a man a woman or a woman a man."

Thus was the notion of legislative sovereignty added to the stock of American political ideas.[134] Its essential contradiction of the elements of theory which had been contributed by earlier thinkers is manifest. What Coke and Locke give us is, for the most part, cautions and safeguards against power; in Blackstone, on the other hand, as in Hobbes, we find the claims of power exalted. This occurred, moreover, at a moment when, as

[131] *Ibid.* 91.   [132] *Ibid.* 161–62.   [133] *Ibid.* 160–61.

[134] Blackstone, however, was not the first to introduce the notion in the Colonies. See some earlier pulpit utterances recorded in BALDWIN, *op. cit. supra* note 93, at 42n. "The Legislature is Accountable to none. There is no Authority above them. . . ."

it happened, not merely the actual structure of government in the United States, but this strong trend of thought among the American people afforded the thesis of legislative sovereignty every promise of easy lodgement.

The formula laid down by the Declaration of Independence regarding the right of revolution is a most conservative one. The right is not to be exercised for "light and transient causes," but only to arrest a settled and deliberate course of tyranny. Yet within a twelve-month of the Declaration we find one Benjamin Hichborn of Boston proclaiming the following doctrine:

I define civil liberty to be not a "government by laws," made agreeable to charters, bills of rights or compacts, but a power existing in the people at large, at any time, for any cause, or for no cause, but their own sovereign pleasure, to alter or annihilate both the mode and essence of any former government, and adopt a new one in its stead.[135]

Ultimately the doctrine of popular sovereignty thus voiced was to be turned against both legislative sovereignty and at a critical moment against state particularism. But at the outset it aided both these ideas, because the state was conceived to stand nearer to the people than the Continental Congress, and because, within the state, the legislature was conceived to stand nearer to the people than the other departments.[136] Thus legislative sovereignty, a derivative from the notion of popular sovereignty in the famous text from Justinian which was quoted at the outset of this study, was recruited afresh from the parent stream, with the result that all the varied rights of man were threatened with submergence in a single right, that of belonging to a popular majority, or more accurately, of being represented by a legislative majority.[137]

[135] NILES, PRINCIPLES AND ACTS 47.

[136] On the growth of particularism, as shown by the proceedings in the Continental Congress, especially regarding the Articles of Confederation, see ADAMS, JUBILEE DISCOURSE ON THE CONSTITUTION (1839) 13 *et seq*.

[137] "The Law of nature is not, as the English utilitarians in their ignorance of its history supposed, a synonym for arbitrary individual preferences, but on the contrary it is a living embodiment of the collective reason

Why, then, did not legislative sovereignty finally establish itself in our constitutional system? To answer at this point solely in terms of institutions, the reason is twofold. In the first place, in the American *written Constitution,* higher law at last attained a form which made possible the attribution to it of an entirely new sort of validity, the validity of a *statute emanating from the sovereign people.* Once the binding force of higher law was transferred to this new basis, the notion of the sovereignty of the ordinary legislative organ disappeared automatically, since that cannot be a *sovereign* law-making body which is subordinate to another law-making body. But in the second place, even statutory form could hardly have saved the higher law as *a recourse for individuals* had it not been backed up by *judicial review.* Invested with statutory form and implemented by judicial review, higher law, as with renewed youth, entered upon one of the great periods of its history, and juristically the most fruitful one since the days of Justinian.

---

of civilized mankind. . . . But it has its limits. . . . Natural justice has no means . . . of choosing one practical solution out of two or more which are in themselves equally plausible. Positive law, whether enacted or customary, must come to our aid in such matters." POLLOCK, EXPANSION OF THE COMMON LAW (1904) 128. The arguments of the analytical school against higher law notions must be conceded to this extent: it is better to confine the term "law" to rules enforced by the state. But that fact does not prove that the term should be applied to all such rules. In urging that it should be, the analytical thinkers endeavor to steal something—they try to transfer to unworthy rules supported by the state the prestige attaching to the word "law" conceived of as the embodiment of justice. The trouble with the analysts, in other words, is not that they define "law" too narrowly, but too broadly.